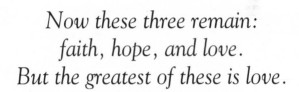

Now these three remain:
faith, hope, and love.
But the greatest of these is love.

—

1 Corinthians 13:1-13 Holman CSB

FAMILY
Christian Stores®

Scripture quotations are taken from:

The Holy Bible, King James Version (KJV)

The Holy Bible, New International Version (NIV) Copyright © 1973, 1978, 1984, by International Bible Society. Used by permission of Zondervan Publishing House. All rights reserved.

The Holy Bible, New King James Version (NKJV) Copyright © 1982 by Thomas Nelson, Inc. Used by permission.

Holy Bible, New Living Translation, (NLT) copyright © 1996. Used by permission of Tyndale House Publishers, Inc., Wheaton, Illinois 60189. All rights reserved.

The Message (MSG)- This edition issued by contractual arrangement with NavPress, a division of The Navigators, U.S.A. Originally published by NavPress in English as THE MESSAGE: The Bible in Contemporary Language copyright 2002-2003 by Eugene Peterson. All rights reserved.

New Century Version®. (NCV) Copyright © 1987, 1988, 1991 by Word Publishing, a division of Thomas Nelson, Inc. All rights reserved. Used by permission.

The New American Standard Bible®, (NASB) Copyright © 1960, 1962, 1963, 1968, 1971, 1972, 1973, 1975, 1977, 1995 by The Lockman Foundation. Used by permission.

The Holman Christian Standard Bible™ (HOLMAN CSB) Copyright © 1999, 2000, 2001 by Holman Bible Publishers. Used by permission.

Cover Design by Kim Russell / Wahoo Designs
Page Layout by Bart Dawsonn

ISBN 978-1-60587-081-6

Printed in the United States of America

Praying for my Wife

100 Daily Devotions for Husbands

PRAYING FOR MY WIFE...100 DAILY DEVOTIONS

PRAYING FOR MY WIFE...100 DAILY DEVOTIONS

PRAYING FOR MY WIFE...100 DAILY DEVOTIONS

PRAYING FOR MY WIFE...100 DAILY DEVOTIONS

Praying for my Wife

100 Daily Devotions for Husbands

PRAYING FOR MY WIFE...100 DAILY DEVOTIONS

PRAYING FOR MY WIFE...100 DAILY DEVOTIONS

PRAYING FOR MY WIFE...100 DAILY DEVOTIONS

Introduction

What's the best thing you can do for your wife? Take her on a big vacation? Plan a romantic dinner? Bring home a dozen roses? Wrong, wrong, and wrong. The best thing you can do for your bride is to pray for her early and often.

How do you and your wife begin the day? Do you awaken early enough to enjoy a few quiet moments together, or are you one of those couples who sleeps until the last possible minute, leaving no time to invest in matters of the heart or the soul? If you and your mate form the habit of getting up early—if both of you start the day by spending a few quiet moments with each other and with God—your marriage will be blessed. After all, the fabric of your marriage is woven together with the threads of habit. And no habit is more important to your family's spiritual health than the habit of daily prayer and devotion to your Creator.

This book contains devotional readings that are intended to help you think about your role as a husband. This text will also help you pray for your wife and for your marriage. So make this promise to yourself, to your wife, and to your God: promise that you will use the ideas on these pages to make your marriage a model of Christian love. Promise, also, that for the next 100 days—and every day thereafter—you will seek God's guidance for your marriage. When you do, your Heavenly Father will bless you and your wife today, tomorrow, and forever.

Day 1

Praying for (and with) Your Wife

The intense prayer of the righteous is very powerful.
James 5:16 Holman CSB

D o you pray for your wife early and often? Do you and your wife "pray without ceasing," or is prayer usually an afterthought? Do you regularly pray together, or do you only bow your heads in unison during Sunday morning services? The answers to these questions determine the quality of your prayer life and, to a surprising extent, the spiritual strength of your marriage.

Andrew Murray observed, "Some people pray just to pray, and some people pray to know God." Your task, along with your wife, is to pray together, not out of habit or obligation, but out of a sincere desire to know your Heavenly Father.

Through constant prayers, you and your bride should petition God, you should praise God, and you should seek God's guidance for your marriage and your life.

Prayer changes things, prayer changes people, and prayer changes marriages. So don't limit your prayers to meals or to bedtime. Pray constantly about things great and small. Pray for your marriage, for your family, and for your wife. God is listening, and He wants to hear from you right now.

Your wife's relationship with God will affect her relationship with you more than anything else.

Stormie Omartian

A beautiful relationship with your mate will enhance your creativity and upgrade your standard of living while improving your quality of life.

Zig Ziglar

Therefore I want the men in every place to pray, lifting up holy hands without anger or argument.

1 Timothy 2:8 Holman CSB

Today's Prayer

Dear Lord, today and every day, I will pray for my wife. Bless her and keep her, Father. I praise You, Lord, for bringing us together. Protect our family and bless our marriage, now and forever. Amen

A Healthy Marriage

What therefore God hath joined together,
let not man put asunder.
Matthew 19:6 KJV

L ove is a journey. A healthy marriage is a lifelong exercise in love, fidelity, trust, understanding, forgiveness, caring, sharing, and encouragement. It requires empathy, tenderness, patience, and perseverance. It is the union of two adults, both of whom are willing to compromise and, when appropriate, to apologize. It requires heaping helpings of common sense, common courtesy, and uncommon caring. A healthy marriage is a joy to behold, an even greater joy to experience . . . and a blessing forever.

The loving relationship between a husband and wife may require the couple to travel together through the dark valleys of disappointment and sorrow, but even on those darkest days, the couple can remain steadfast . . . if they choose to follow God.

As we make our daily journey with God, we travel through a world that presents us with countless temptations to stray far from His path. So we must be watchful, we must be thoughtful, and we must be obedient to God.

When we behave ourselves as obedient servants, we honor the Father and the Son. When we live righteously and according to God's commandments, we build better marriages and better lives. When we obey God, He blesses us in ways that we cannot fully understand. So, as this day unfolds, take every step of your journey with God as your traveling companion. Study His Holy Word. Follow His commandments. Support only those activities that further God's kingdom and your spiritual growth. Be an example of righteous living to your neighbors, to your children, and to your wife. And make certain that you keep God where He belongs: at the center of all your relationships, including your marriage.

Marriage is a divine institution, founded by God. Society did not make the first marriage; God did.

Billy Graham

Today's Prayer

We pray to You, Father, because You desire it and because we need it. Prayer not only changes things, it changes us. And it can change our marriage. Help us, Lord, never to face the demands of the day without first spending time with You, and bless our marriage today, tomorrow, and forever. Amen

You Are Blessed

*He who finds a wife finds what is good
and receives favor from the Lord.*
Proverbs 18:22 NIV

Your life and your marriage are gifts from God; celebrate those blessings and give thanks. And make no mistake: When you celebrate the gifts of life and love, your thankful heart will serve as a powerful blessing to your bride.

Every good gift comes from God. As believers who have been saved by a risen Christ, we owe unending thanksgiving to our Heavenly Father. Yet sometimes, amid the crush of everyday living, we simply don't stop long enough to pause and thank our Creator for His countless blessings. As Christians, we are blessed beyond measure. Thus, thanksgiving should become a habit, a regular part of our daily routines.

Thoughtful husbands can face the inevitable challenges of married life armed with the joy of Christ and the promise of salvation. So whatever this day holds for you, begin it and end it with God as your partner and Christ as your Savior. And throughout the day, give thanks to the One who created you and saved you. Place

God squarely at the center of your marriage and your life. Then celebrate! God's love for you is infinite. Accept it joyously and be thankful.

God wants his people to earnestly seek his will and to pray for it, and thus to become agents of the blessing God brings.

James Montgomery Boice

Think of the blessings we so easily take for granted: Life itself; preservation from danger; every bit of health we enjoy; every hour of liberty; the ability to see, to hear, to speak, to think, and to imagine all this comes from the hand of God.

Billy Graham

I will bless them and the places surrounding my hill. I will send down showers in season; there will be showers of blessings.

Ezekiel 34:26 NIV

Today's Prayer

Dear Lord, You have given us so much, and we are thankful. We know that every good gift is to be shared with others. We give thanks for Your gifts . . . and we will share them. Amen

Putting God First

You shall have no other gods before Me.
Exodus 20:3 NKJV

D o you and your wife put God first in your marriage? Or do you allow yourselves to be hijacked by the inevitable obligations and distractions of 21st-century life? When you and your beloved allow Christ to reign over your lives and your marriage, your household will be eternally blessed.

God loved this world so much that He sent His Son to save it. And now only one real question remains: what will you and yours do in response to God's love? The answer should be obvious: You must put God first in every aspect of your lives, including your marriage.

God is with you always, listening to your thoughts and prayers, watching over your every move. As the demands of everyday life weigh down upon you, you may be tempted to ignore God's presence or—worse yet—to rebel against His commandments. But, when you quiet yourself and acknowledge His presence, God touches your heart and restores your spirits.

At this very moment, God is seeking to work in you and through you. So why not let Him do it right now?

A man's spiritual health is exactly proportional to his love for God.

C. S. Lewis

You must never sacrifice your relationship with God for the sake of a relationship with another person.

Charles Stanley

Make God's will the focus of your life day by day. If you seek to please Him and Him alone, you'll find yourself satisfied with life.

Kay Arthur

It is impossible to please God doing things motivated by and produced by the flesh.

Bill Bright

Be careful not to forget the Lord.

Deuteronomy 6:12 Holman CSB

Today's Prayer

Dear Lord, we know that when we put You first, we are blessed. Keep us mindful that we must put You first and keep You first today, tomorrow, and every day that we live. Amen

Day 5

The Greatest of These

Now these three remain: faith, hope, and love.
But the greatest of these is love.

1 Corinthians 13:13 Holman CSB

As a thoughtful husband, you understand the crucial role that love does play—and should play—in every marriage, including your own. And the familiar words of 1st Corinthians 13 serve as a beautiful reminder of the importance and the power of love. Yet sometimes, amid the inevitable struggles of everyday life, you may lose sight—at least temporarily—of the love you feel for your wife.

Christ showed His love for us on the cross, and, as Christians we are called to return Christ's love by sharing it. And Paul instructed husbands to love their wives in the same way that Christ loved His church: "Husbands, love your wives, just as also Christ loved the church and gave Himself for her" (Ephesians 5:25 Holman CSB).

Sometimes, of course, love is easy (puppies and sleeping children come to mind), and sometimes love is hard (imperfect husbands and wives come to mind). But God's Word is clear: We are to love our wives (and everyone for that matter) at all times, not just when they seem most lovable.

So do the right thing: Tell your wife that you love her every chance you get. Tell her in person; call her on the phone; leave her notes; give her encouragement, cooperation, and praise. Demonstrate your love with words and deeds—your wife needs both . . . and she deserves both.

The cross symbolizes a cosmic as well as a historic truth. Love conquers the world, but its victory is not an easy one.

Reinhold Neibuhr

The one who does not love does not know God, because God is love.

1 John 4:8 Holman CSB

Today's Prayer

Dear Lord, You have given us the gift of eternal love; let my wife and I share that gift with each other and with the world. Help us, Father, to show kindness to those who cross our path, and let us show tenderness and unfailing love to our family and friends. Make us generous with words of encouragement and praise. And, help us always to reflect the love that Christ has given us, so that through us, others might find Him. Amen

Day 6

Asking for Directions

If you need wisdom—if you want to know what
God wants you to do—ask him, and he will gladly tell you.
He will not resent your asking.

James 1:5 NLT

How often do you and your wife ask for God's help? Occasionally? Intermittently? Whenever you experience a crisis? Hopefully not. Hopefully, you have developed the habit of asking for God's assistance early and often. And hopefully, you have learned to seek His guidance in every aspect of your life.

God has promised that when you ask for His help, He will not withhold it. So ask. Ask Him to meet the needs of your day. Ask Him for wisdom. Ask Him to lead you, to protect you, and to correct you. And trust the answers He gives.

God stands at the door and waits. When you knock on His door, He answers. Your task, of course, is to seek His guidance prayerfully, confidently, and often.

Notice that we must ask. And we will sometimes struggle to hear and struggle with what we hear. But personally, it's worth it. I'm after the path of life—and he alone knows it.

John Eldredge

Aspire to God with short but frequent outpourings of the heart; admire His bounty; invoke His aid; cast yourself in spirit at the foot of His cross; adore His goodness; give Him your whole soul a thousand times in the day.

St. Francis of Sales

You need not cry very loudly: he is nearer to us than we think.

Brother Lawrence

Until now you have asked for nothing in My name. Ask and you will receive, that your joy may be complete.

John 16:24 Holman CSB

Today's Prayer

Dear Lord, You are the giver of all things good. When my wife and I are in need, we will come to You in prayer. You know the desires of our hearts, Lord; grant them, we ask. Yet not our will, Father, but Your will be done. Amen

Day 7

Total Commitment

Marriage should be honored by everyone, and husband and wife should keep their marriage pure.

Hebrews 13:4 NCV

In a good marriage, the words "love" and "commitment" are intertwined. According to God, genuine love is patient, unselfish, and kind, but it goes beyond that—genuine love is committed love, and that means that genuine love is more than a feeling . . . it is a decision to make love endure, no matter what.

Unfortunately, we live in a world where marriage vows are sometimes taken far too lightly. Too many couples are far too quick to push the panic button—or the eject button—and the results are predictably tragic.

As a married man who has vowed to love your wife "till death do you part," you must take that vow very seriously. Your wife must know, beyond any doubt, that you are totally committed to her, totally committed to your family, and totally committed to your marriage. How can you do it? The best place to start is by putting God right where He belongs: at the absolute center of your family and your marriage.

When you and your spouse worship God together, you'll soon notice a change in your relationship. When the two of you sincerely embrace God's love, you will feel differently about yourself, your marriage, your family, and your world. When you and your spouse embrace God's love together, your marriage will be transformed. And, when the two of you accept the Father's grace and share His love, you will be blessed here on earth and throughout eternity.

So, if you genuinely seek to build a marriage that will stand the test of time, make God the foundation. When you do, your love will endure for a lifetime and beyond.

Marital love is a committed act of the will before it is anything else. It is sacrificial love, a no-turning-back decision.

Ed Young

To sum up, each one of you is to love his wife as himself, and the wife is to respect her husband.

Ephesians 5:33 Holman CSB

Today's Prayer

Dear Lord, Your Word teaches us that our marriage is both sacred and eternal. We thank You, Father, for the love that we share today, tomorrow, and forever. Amen

The Morning Watch

Every morning he wakes me. He teaches me to listen
like a student. The Lord God helps me learn . . .
Isaiah 50:4-5 NCV

E ach new day is a gift from God, and if you are wise,
you will spend a few quiet moments each morning
thanking the Giver.

Warren Wiersbe writes, "Surrender your mind to the
Lord at the beginning of each day." And that's sound
advice. When you begin each day with your head bowed
and your heart lifted, you are reminded of God's love, His
protection, and His commandments. Then, you can align
your priorities for the coming day with the teachings and
commandments that God has placed upon your heart.

How do you and your wife prepare for the day ahead? Do
you awaken early enough to spend at least a few moments
with God? Or do you both sleep until the last possible
minute, leaving no time to invest in matters of the heart
and soul? Hopefully, you make a habit of spending precious
moments each morning with your Creator. When you do,
He will fill your hearts, He will direct your thoughts, and
He will guide your steps.

Your daily devotional time can be habit-forming, and should be. The first few minutes of each day are invaluable. Treat them that way, and offer them to God.

I suggest you discipline yourself to spend time daily in a systematic reading of God's Word. Make this "quiet time" a priority that nobody can change.

Warren Wiersbe

If thou may not continually gather thyself together, do it some time at least, once a day, morning or evening.

Thomas á Kempis

Every morning I spend fifteen minutes filling my mind full of God; and so there's no room left for worry.

Howard Chandler Christy

Today's Prayer

Dear Lord, my wife and I come to You for guidance, for perspective, for wisdom, and for protection. Lead us, Father, this day and every day as we seek to obey Your Word and to honor Your Son. Amen

The Power of Encouragement

Therefore encourage one another and build each other up as you are already doing.

1 Thessalonians 5:11 Holman CSB

Marriage is a team sport, and all of us need occasional pats on the back from our teammate. In the Book of Proverbs, we read that, "A word aptly spoken is like apples of gold in settings of silver" (25:11 NIV). This verse reminds us that the words we speak can and should be beautiful offerings to those we love.

All of us have the power to enrich the lives of our loved ones. Sometimes, when we feel uplifted and secure, we find it easy to speak words of encouragement and hope. Other times, when we are discouraged or tired, we can scarcely summon the energy to uplift ourselves, much less anyone else. But, as loving Christians, our obligation is clear: we must always measure our words carefully as we use them to benefit others and to glorify our Father.

God intends that we speak words of kindness, wisdom, and truth, no matter our circumstances, no matter our emotions. When we do, we share a priceless gift with our loved ones, and we give glory to the One who gave His life for us. As believers, we must do no less.

The truest help we can render an afflicted man is not to take his burden from him, but to call out his best energy, that he may be able to bear the burden himself.

Phillips Brooks

Isn't it funny the way some combinations of words can give you—almost apart from their meaning—a thrill like music?

C. S. Lewis

I want their hearts to be encouraged and joined together in love, so that they may have all the riches of assured understanding, and have the knowledge of God's mystery—Christ.

Colossians 2:2 Holman CSB

Today's Prayer

Dear Lord, make me a man who is quick to celebrate the accomplishments of others. Make me a source of genuine, lasting encouragement to my wife, to my family, to my friends, and to the world. And let my words and deeds be worthy of Your Son, the One who gives me strength and salvation, this day and for all eternity. Amen

Partners in Growth

But grow in the grace and knowledge of our Lord
and Savior Jesus Christ. To Him be the glory both
now and to the day of eternity.

2 Peter 3:18 Holman CSB

At its best, a Christian marriage is this: a partnership between two believers who embark upon a lifelong journey toward spiritual maturity and growth. No Christian couple should ever be completely satisfied with the condition of their spiritual health; instead, they should continue to grow in the love and the knowledge of their Savior.

When we cease to grow, either emotionally or spiritually, we do ourselves and our loved ones a profound disservice. But, if we study God's Word, if we obey His commandments, and if we live in the center of His will, we will not be stagnant believers; we will, instead, be growing Christians . . . and that's exactly what God wants for our marriages and our lives.

Does your wife encourage your spiritual growth, and is the reverse also true? If so, you are to be congratulated. If not, it's time for change. After all, God doesn't want you (or your marriage) to be stagnant. He wants you to keep growing and growing. And that's exactly what you should want, too.

We often become mentally and spiritually barren because we're so busy.

Franklin Graham

The vigor of our spiritual lives will be in exact proportion to the place held by the Bible in our lives and in our thoughts.

George Mueller

God's plan for our guidance is for us to grow gradually in wisdom before we get to the crossroads.

Bill Hybels

Leave inexperience behind, and you will live; pursue the way of understanding.

Proverbs 9:6 Holman CSB

Today's Prayer

Dear Lord, help us to keep growing spiritually and emotionally. Let us live according to Your Word, and let us grow in our faith every day that we live. Amen

This Is His Day

This is the day the LORD has made.
We will rejoice and be glad in it.
Psalm 118:24 NLT

G od gives us this day; He fills it to the brim with possibilities, and He challenges us to use it for His purposes. The 118th Psalm reminds us that today, like every other day, is a cause for celebration. The day is presented to us fresh and clean at midnight, free of charge, but we must beware: Today is a non-renewable resource—once it's gone, it's gone forever. Our responsibility, of course, is to use this day in the service of God's will and according to His commandments.

Christ made it clear to His followers: He intended that His joy would become their joy. And it still holds true today: Christ intends that His believers share His love with joy in their hearts. Yet sometimes, amid the inevitable hustle and bustle of life here on earth, we can forfeit—albeit temporarily—the joy of Christ as we wrestle with the challenges of daily living.

Joy is an important part of healthy Christian relationships. Joyful believers tend to form joyful relationships, and that's exactly what God intends.

Are you doing your best to live each day as a joyful servant of Christ? And, are you inviting your wife to join in the celebration? Hopefully so. After all, few things in life are more wonderful to behold than the joining together of two joyful believers. So now, with no further ado, thank God for your marriage, and let the celebration begin!

Joy is not the same as happiness—although they may overlap. Happiness depends on circumstances; joy depends on God.

Billy Graham

Some of us seem so anxious about avoiding hell that we forget to celebrate our journey toward heaven.

Philip Yancey

Always be full of joy in the Lord. I say it again—rejoice!

Philippians 4:4 NLT

Today's Prayer

Lord, You are the Giver of all life, and You have created us to have fellowship with You. Let my wife and I live lives that are pleasing to You. We will celebrate together, Father, and we will give thanks for Your blessings today and throughout all eternity. Amen

Best Friends

If we love one another, God abides in us,
and His love is perfected in us.
1 John 4:12 NASB

What is a friend? The dictionary defines the word "friend" as "a person who is attached to another by feelings of affection or personal regard." This definition is accurate, as far as it goes, but when we examine the deeper meaning of friendship, especially as it applies to our loved ones, so many more descriptors apply: trustworthiness, loyalty, helpfulness, kindness, understanding, forgiveness, encouragement, humor, and cheerfulness, to mention but a few.

The best marriages are built upon love and friendship. Is your spouse your best friend? Hopefully this is the case. If so, you are immensely blessed by God—and you must never take His gift for granted.

But if you find yourself placing other friendships above the friendship you share with your spouse, it's time to have a serious talk with the person you see every time you look into the mirror.

Friendship should be an important element of any marriage, including yours. So, if you'd like a proven prescription for marital bliss, here it is: make sure that your spouse is also your closest friend and most trusted confidante. If that advice sounds simple, it is. But it's also advice that, if taken to heart, can bring lasting joy to you and yours.

Marriage is God's idea. He "crafted" it. If your marriage is broken, all the "repairmen" or counselors or seminars you take it to will be unable to fix it; take it to Him. The Creator who made it in the first place can make it work again.

Anne Graham Lotz

Cooperation is a two-way street, but for too many couples, it's the road less traveled.

Marie T. Freeman

Now these three remain: faith, hope, and love. But the greatest of these is love.

1 Corinthians 13:13 Holman CSB

Today's Prayer

Dear Lord, as we build our marriage day by day, we will build it upon friendship and upon trust—trust in each other and trust in You. Amen

An Attitude of Gratitude

Finally brothers, whatever is true, whatever is honorable,
whatever is just, whatever is pure, whatever is lovely,
whatever is commendable—if there is any moral excellence
and if there is any praise—dwell on these things.
Philippians 4:8 Holman CSB

A Christian marriage should be cause for celebration, but sometimes we don't feel much like celebrating. In fact, when the weight of the world seems to bear down upon our shoulders, celebration may be the last thing on our minds . . . but it shouldn't be. As God's children, we are all blessed beyond measure on good days and bad. This day is a non-renewable resource— once it's gone, it's gone forever. We should give thanks for this day while using it for the glory of God.

What will be your attitude today? Will you be fearful, angry, bored, or worried? Will you infect your marriage with the twin blights of cynicism and negativity? Or will you choose to be a better man, a man who decides, instead, to celebrate your life and your loved ones? The choice is yours, and so are the consequences.

Please remember that God has richly blessed you, and

He wants you to rejoice in His gifts. But, He will not force His joy upon you; you must claim it for yourself.

So today, and every day hereafter, celebrate the life that God has given you. Think optimistically about yourself, your marriage, your family, and your future. Look for goodness, not faults; look for strengths, not shortcomings. And vow to be a positive influence on everybody you meet, starting with your bride. She deserves that kind of husband. And you deserve the rewards that inevitably come to men (like you) who learn how to count—and how to keep counting—their blessings.

The life of strain is difficult. The life of inner peace—a life that comes from a positive attitude—is the easiest type of existence.

Norman Vincent Peale

Set your minds on what is above, not on what is on the earth.

Colossians 3:2 Holman CSB

Today's Prayer

Dear Lord, help me have an attitude that is pleasing to You and helpful to my family as I count my blessings today, tomorrow, and every day. Amen

Day 14

Your Traveling Companion

But thanks be to God, who gives us the victory through our Lord Jesus Christ. Therefore, my beloved brethren, be steadfast, immovable, always abounding in the work of the Lord, knowing that your labor is not in vain in the Lord.

1 Corinthians 15:57-58 NKJV

Your wife needs to know that you love her today, that you will love her tomorrow, and that you will love her forever. Marriage is, after all, a marathon, not a sprint—and couples who expect otherwise will be sadly disappointed. That's why husbands and wives need large quantities of patience, forgiveness, hope, and perseverance.

Every marriage and every life has its share of roadblocks and stumbling blocks; these situations require courage and determination. As an example of perfect courage and steadfast determination, we need look no further than our Savior, Jesus Christ.

Jesus finished what He began. Despite the torture He endured, despite the shame of the cross, Jesus was steadfast in His faithfulness to God. We, too, must remain faithful—

faithful to God, faithful to our principles, and faithful to our loved ones—especially during times of transition or hardship.

The next time you are tempted to give up on yourself, your duties, or your relationships, ask yourself this question: "What would Jesus have me do?" When you find the answer to that question, you'll know precisely what to do.

By perseverance the snail reached the ark.

C. H. Spurgeon

When you persevere through a trial, God gives you a special measure of insight.

Charles Swindoll

So we must not get tired of doing good, for we will reap at the proper time if we don't give up.

Galatians 6:9 Holman CSB

Today's Prayer

Dear Lord, when my wife and I are discouraged, we will turn to You for strength, courage, and faith. Today and every day, we will look to You as the ultimate source of our hope, our strength, our peace, and our salvation. Amen

Day 15

God's Guidance

The steps of the Godly are directed by God.
He delights in every detail of their lives.
Psalm 37:22 NLT

God is intensely interested in each of us, and He will guide our steps if we serve Him obediently. When we sincerely offer heartfelt prayers to our Heavenly Father, He will give direction and meaning to our lives—but He won't force us to follow Him. To the contrary, God has given us the free will to follow His commandments . . . or not.

When we stray from God's commandments, we invite bitter consequences. But, when we follow His commandments, and when we genuinely and humbly seek His will, He touches our hearts and leads us on the path of His choosing.

Will you trust God to manage your life and your marriage? You should. When you entrust your life to Him completely and without reservation, God will give you the strength to meet any challenge, the courage to face any trial, and the wisdom to live in His righteousness and in His peace. So trust Him today and seek His guidance. When you do, your next step will be the right one.

A spiritual discipline is necessary in order to move slowly from an absurd life to an obedient life, from a life filled with noisy worries to a life in which there is some free inner space where we can listen to our God and follow his guidance.

Henri Nouwen

Only He can guide you to invest your life in worthwhile ways. This guidance will come as you "walk" with Him and listen to Him.

Henry Blackaby and Claude King

I don't doubt that the Holy Spirit guides your decisions from within when you make them with the intention of pleasing God. The error would be to think that He speaks only within, whereas in reality He speaks also through Scripture, the Church, Christian friends, and books.

C. S. Lewis

Lord, You are my lamp; the Lord illuminates my darkness.

2 Samuel 22:29 Holman CSB

Today's Prayer

Dear Lord, You always stand ready to guide us. Let us accept Your guidance, today and every day of our lives. Lead us, Father, so that our lives can be a tribute to Your grace, to Your mercy, to Your love, and to Your Son. Amen

Dreaming About an Intensely Bright Future: Yours

I came so they can have real and eternal life,
more and better life than they ever dreamed of.
John 10:10 MSG

D o you and your wife spend time together planning for the future and sharing your dreams? And, are you willing to entertain the possibility that God has big plans in store for your marriage? Hopefully so. Yet sometimes, especially if you've recently experienced a life-altering disappointment, you may find it difficult to envision a brighter future for yourself or your family. If so, it's time to reconsider your own capabilities . . . and God's.

Your Heavenly Father created you and your loved ones with unique gifts and untapped talents; your job is to tap them. When you do, you'll begin to feel an increasing sense of confidence in yourself and in your future.

It takes courage to dream big dreams and even more courage to share them. You will discover that kind of courage when you do three things: accept the past, trust God to handle the future, and make the most of the time

He has given you today. Nothing is too difficult for God, and no dreams are too big for Him—not even yours. So start living—and dreaming—accordingly.

Dreams are wonderful things to share with your wife. Have you shared yours lately? Hopefully so. But if you've been hesitant to give voice to your hopes and plans, remember this: dreaming works best when it's a team sport.

You cannot out-dream God.

John Eldredge

The biggest human temptation is to settle for too little.

Thomas Merton

Now may the God of hope fill you with all joy and peace in believing, so that you may overflow with hope by the power of the Holy Spirit.

Romans 15:13 Holman CSB

Today's Prayer

Dear Lord, give us the courage to dream and the faithfulness to trust in Your perfect plan. When my wife and I are worried or weary, give us strength for today and hope for tomorrow. Keep us mindful of Your infinite love, Your healing power, and Your glorious plans for us today, tomorrow, and forever. Amen

Day 17

The Art of Listening

My dearly loved brothers, understand this: everyone must be quick to hear, slow to speak, and slow to anger.

James 1:19 Holman CSB

What a blessing it is when our loved ones genuinely seek to understand who we are and what we think. Just as we wish to be understood by others, so, too, should we seek to understand the hopes and dreams of our spouses and our family members.

Are you in the habit of listening to your wife? Do you listen carefully (not superficially), and do you take time to think about the things she says? If so, you're building a stronger marriage. But if you allow the obligations of everyday living to interfere with the communications you share with your mate, it's time to reorder your priorities.

You live in a busy world, a place where it is all too easy to overlook the needs of others, but God's Word instructs you to do otherwise. In the Gospel of Matthew, Jesus declares, "In everything, therefore, treat people the same way you want them to treat you, for this is the Law and the Prophets" (Matthew 7:12 NASB). This is the Golden Rule, and it should govern your marriage.

Do you want your voice to be heard? Of course you do. So, in adherence with the Golden Rule, you should also let your wife's voice be heard, too—heard by you.

The cliché is true: People don't care what we know until they know we care.

Rick Warren

Listening is loving.

Zig Ziglar

One of the best ways to encourage someone who's hurting is with your ears—by listening.

Barbara Johnson

A wise man will hear and increase learning.

Proverbs 1:5 NKJV

Today's Prayer

Dear Lord, let us listen carefully to each other and to You. When we listen, we learn. So, today and every day, let us strive to understand each other as we follow in the footsteps of Your Son. Amen

Your Family: A Gift from God

*Choose for yourselves today the one you will worship . . . .
As for me and my family, we will worship the Lord.*
Joshua 24:15 Holman CSB

As a thoughtful husband, you know that your family is a priceless treasure from God. And if you're a wise husband, you'll make certain that your wife knows that you know. How? By telling her how thankful you are for the gift of family, that's how.

But sometimes, you'll be tempted to rush through life while giving little notice to your blessings. After all, if you're a busy husband working in a demanding world, the pressures can be intense. As those pressures build, you may tend to focus so intently upon your obligations to your family that you forget to give thanks for your family. But to do so is a big mistake. So even when the demands of everyday life are great, you must never forget that you have been entrusted with a profound responsibility: the responsibility of contributing to your family's emotional and spiritual well-being. It's a big job, but with God's help, you're up to the task.

When you place God squarely in the center of your family's life—when you worship Him, praise Him, trust Him, and love Him—then He will most certainly bless you and yours in ways that you could have scarcely imagined.

So the next time your family life becomes a little stressful, remember this: That little band of men, women, kids, and babies is a priceless treasure on temporary loan from the Father above. And it's your responsibility to praise God for that gift—and to act accordingly.

Love is most often found in the home—in the presence of a caring and considerate mate who nurtures love daily.

Zig Ziglar

If a kingdom is divided against itself, that kingdom cannot stand. If a house is divided against itself, that house cannot stand.

Mark 3:24-25 Holman CSB

Today's Prayer

Dear Lord, we are part of Your family, and we praise You for Your gifts and for Your love. You have also blessed us with our own earthly family, and we pray for them, that they might be protected and blessed by You. Let us show love and acceptance for our family, Lord, so that through us, they might come to know You and to love You. Amen

Always Praising Him

Through Him then, let us continually offer up
a sacrifice of praise to God, that is,
the fruit of lips that give thanks to His name.
Hebrews 13:15 NASB

I t's easy to "compartmentalize" our waking hours into a few familiar categories: work, rest, play, family time, and worship. As creatures of habit, we may find ourselves praising God only at particular times of the day or on a particular day of the week. But praise for our Creator should never be reserved for mealtimes, bedtimes, or church. Instead, we should praise God all day, every day, to the greatest extent we can, with thanksgiving in our hearts, and with a song on our lips.

Worship and praise should be woven into the fabric of everything we do; they should not be relegated to a weekly three-hour visit to church on Sunday morning. A. W. Tozer correctly observed, "If you will not worship God seven days a week, you do not worship Him on one day a week."

Do you praise God many times each day? And do you thank Him specifically for your wife and family?

If so, keep up the good work; if not, it's time to reassess your priorities. When you consider the wonderful things that God has done for you, you'll find the time—or more accurately you'll make the time—to praise Him for all that He has done.

Every time you notice a gift from the Creator, thank Him and praise Him. His works are marvelous, His gifts are beyond understanding, and His love endures forever.

Be not afraid of saying too much in the praises of God; all the danger is of saying too little.

Matthew Henry

Praise him, all you people of the earth, for he loves us with unfailing love; the faithfulness of the Lord endures forever. Praise the Lord!

Psalm 117 NLT

Today's Prayer

Dear Lord, sometimes, amid the demands of the day, we lose perspective, and we fail to give thanks for Your blessings and for Your love. Today, help us count those blessings, and let us give thanks to You, Father, for Your love, for Your grace, for Your blessings, and for Your Son. Amen

Sharing His Joy

Be happy with the wife you married when you were young.
She gives you joy, as your fountain gives you water.

Proverbs 5:18 NCV

Does your wife know that she brings you great joy? Do you tell her so? And do you show her, by your words and your actions, that you are a joyful man, a man who appreciates God's blessings? Hopefully so. After all, you and your wife have many reasons to be grateful: God is in His heaven; Christ has risen, and you are the sheep of His flock. And, God has brought the two of you together, not just for a lifetime, but for eternity. So what's not to celebrate? Yet sometimes, even the most devout couples may become discouraged. After all, we live in a world where expectations can be high and demands can be even higher.

When we fail to meet the expectations of others (or, for that matter, the expectations that we have for ourselves), we may be tempted to abandon hope. But God has other plans. He knows exactly how He intends to use us. Our task is to remain faithful until He does.

If you or your wife become discouraged by the direction of life, turn your thoughts and prayers to God. He is a God of possibility, not negativity. He will help you count your blessings instead of your hardships. Then, with a renewed spirit of optimism and hope, you can properly thank your Father in heaven for His blessings, for His love, and for His Son.

Your wife will prove to be your greatest asset if you value and honor her.

Stormie Omartian

The mind is like a clock that is constantly running down. It has to be wound up daily with good thoughts.

Fulton J. Sheen

These things I have spoken to you, that My joy may remain in you, and that your joy may be full.

John 15:11 NKJV

Today's Prayer

Dear Lord, You have given us so many blessings; let us celebrate Your gifts. Make us thankful, loving, responsible, and wise. We praise You, Father, for the gift of Your Son and for the priceless gift of salvation. Make us joyful Christians, make us worthy examples to others, and make us dutiful servants to You, now and forever. Amen

Contagious Enthusiasm

Whatever you do, work at it with all your heart,
as working for the Lord, not for men.

Colossians 3:23 NIV

Are you genuinely excited about your marriage? Do you feel good about yourself, your wife, your kids, and your home life? And do you see each day as a glorious opportunity for your family to serve God and to do His will? Hopefully so. After all, you and your family members were created in God's image, and He has blessed you in more ways than you can count. Now, it's your job to thank Him with words and with deeds.

Psalm 100 reminds us that, as believers, we have every reason to celebrate: "Shout for joy to the LORD, all the earth. Worship the LORD with gladness" vv. 1-2 NIV). And as you consider the treasures that God has given you—starting with (but not limited to) your marriage and your family—give thanks to your Creator. And when you're finished thanking your Father in heaven, give thanks to your spouse!

There seems to be a chilling fear of holy enthusiasm among the people of God. We try to tell how happy we are—but we remain so well-controlled that there are very few waves of glory experienced in our midst.

A. W. Tozer

Your enthusiasm will be infectious, stimulating, and attractive to others. They will love you for it. They will go for you and with you.

Norman Vincent Peale

Catch on fire with enthusiasm and people will come for miles to watch you burn.

John Wesley

So, my dear brothers and sisters, be strong and steady, always enthusiastic about the Lord's work, for you know that nothing you do for the Lord is ever useless.

1 Corinthians 15:58 NLT

Today's Prayer

Dear Lord, I know that my wife and family members are watching the way that I live my life. Help me to be an enthusiastic Christian with a faith that is contagious. Amen.

His Promises

Let's keep a firm grip on the promises that keep us going.
He always keeps his word.

Hebrews 10:23 MSG

I s your marriage built upon the foundation of God's promises? Hopefully so. A Christ-centered marriage is a joy to behold, a joy to experience, and a blessing forever.

A Christ-centered marriage is an exercise in faith, love, fidelity, trust, understanding, forgiveness, caring, sharing, and encouragement. It requires empathy, tenderness, patience, and perseverance. It is the union of two Christian adults, both of whom are willing to compromise and, when appropriate, to apologize. A Christ-centered marriage requires heaping helpings of common sense, common courtesy, and uncommon caring.

Does Christ truly preside over your marriage, or does He occupy a position of lesser importance? The answer to that question will determine the quality and direction of your marriage. When both you and your wife allow Jesus to reign over your lives, Christ will bless you and your family in wonderful, unexpected ways. So today and every day, make your marriage a model of Christian love, respect, and service. Trust God's Word and expect Him to fulfill His promises. And rest assured: when you do your part, God will do His part.

We can have full confidence in God's promises because we can have full faith in His character.

Franklin Graham

The stars may fall, but God's promises will stand and be fulfilled.

J. I. Packer

As for God, his way is perfect. All the LORD's promises prove true. He is a shield for all who look to him for protection.

Psalm 18:30 NLT

Today's Prayer

Heavenly Father, when we are troubled, give us hope. When we are weak, give us strength. When we are fearful, let us feel Your healing touch. Let us trust in Your promises, Lord, and let us draw strength from those promises and from Your unending love. Amen

In Times of Adversity

When you go through deep waters and great trouble, I will be with you. When you go through the rivers of difficulty, you will not drown! When you walk through the fire of oppression, you will not be burned up; the flames will not consume you. For I am the Lord, your God . . . .

Isaiah 43:2-3 NLT

Life is a tapestry of good days and difficult days, with the good days predominating. When times are good, we are tempted to take our blessings for granted. But, when times are tough, we discover precisely what we're made of.

Every marriage, like every life, will encounter days of hardship and pain. It is only then that husbands and wives can discover precisely what their marriage is made of.

When we experience a deeply significant loss, we must learn (once again) to trust God and to trust those who love us most. When we do, we come to understand that our suffering carries with it great potential: the potential for intense personal growth and the potential to add depth and meaning to our relationships.

Are you and your wife enduring tough times? If so, hold tightly to each other and turn your hearts toward

God. When you do, you may rest assured that the two of you—plus God—can handle anything that comes your way.

The closer we are to God, the more confidence we place in him when we are under fire.

C. H. Spurgeon

Sometimes your medicine bottle says, "Shake well before using." That is what God has to do with some of his people. He has to shake them well before they are usable.

Vance Havner

Mighty waters cannot extinguish love; rivers cannot sweep it away.

Song of Solomon 8:7 Holman CSB

Today's Prayer

Heavenly Father, You are a refuge for my wife and I. As we journey through this day, we know that we may encounter disappointments and losses. When we are troubled, let us turn to You. Keep us steady, Lord, and renew a right spirit inside our hearts this day and forever. Amen

Measuring Your Words

From a wise mind comes wise speech;
the words of the wise are persuasive.

Proverbs 16:23 NLT

Your skills as a communicator will have a profound impact upon your relationships, starting with that most important relationship: your marriage. Here are a few simple rules that can help: 1. Think First, Speak Second: If you blurt out the first thing that comes into your head, you may say things that are better left unsaid. 2. Learn to Be a Good Listener: Far too many marriages are unsuccessful because one or both spouses simply don't make the effort to listen. If you want your marriage to flourish, listen carefully to your spouse. 3. Don't Be a Chronic Complainer: You'll never whine your way to a happy marriage, so don't even try. 4. Be a Trustworthy Communicator: Don't hedge the truth, don't omit important facts, and don't make promises that you can't keep. 5. Be Encouraging: You should be your spouse's biggest booster, not your spouse's constant critic.

God's Word reminds us that "Reckless words pierce like a sword, but the tongue of the wise brings healing"

(Proverbs 12:18 NIV). So, if you seek to be a source of encouragement to your loved ones, you must measure your words carefully. You must speak wisely, not impulsively. You must use words of kindness and praise, not words of anger or derision. And, you must learn how to be truthful without being cruel.

You have the power to lift your loved ones up or to hold them back. When you learn how to lift them up, you'll soon discover that you've lifted yourself up, too.

Attitude and the spirit in which we communicate are as important as the words we say.

Charles Stanley

A word fitly spoken is like apples of gold in settings of silver.

Proverbs 25:11 NKJV

Today's Prayer

Lord, You have warned me that I will be judged by the words I speak. Keep me mindful, Father, that I have influence on many people; make me an influence for good. Give me wisdom whenever I speak to my wife, to my family, or to my friends. And let the words that I speak today be worthy of the One who has saved me forever. Amen

Day 25

Actions That Reflect Our Beliefs

But prove yourselves doers of the word,
and not merely hearers.
James 1:22 NASB

Are you the kind of practical Christian husband who is willing to dig in and do what needs to be done when it needs to be done? If so, congratulations: God acknowledges your service and blesses it. But if you find yourself more interested in the fine points of theology than in the needs of your neighbors, it's time to rearrange your priorities.

As Christians, we must do our best to ensure that our actions are accurate reflections of our beliefs. Our theology must be demonstrated, not only by our words but, more importantly, by our actions. In short, we should be practical believers, quick to act whenever we see an opportunity to serve God.

God needs believers who are willing to roll up their sleeves and go to work for Him. Count yourself among that number. Theology is a good thing unless it interferes with God's work. And it's up to you to make certain that your theology doesn't.

Do noble things, do not dream them all day long.

Charles Kingsley

Action springs not from thought, but from a readiness for responsibility.

Dietrich Bonhoeffer

Let us not be content to wait and see what will happen, but give us the determination to make the right things happen.

Peter Marshall

It is by acts and not by ideas that people live.

Harry Emerson Fosdick

If the way you live isn't consistent with what you believe, then it's wrong.

Romans 14:23 MSG

Today's Prayer

Heavenly Father, I believe in You, and I believe in Your Word. Help me to live in such a way that my actions validate my beliefs—and as I support my wife and family, let the glory be Yours forever. Amen

A Book Unlike Any Other

*For I am not ashamed of the gospel, because it is
God's power for salvation to everyone who believes.*
Romans 1:16 Holman CSB

Wise Christian couples understand the transforming power of God's Holy Word. The Bible is unlike any other book. It is a priceless gift from our Creator, a tool that God intends for us to use in every aspect of our lives. And, it contains promises upon which we, as Christians, can and must depend.

D. L. Moody advised, "The Bible was not given to increase our knowledge but to change our lives." God's Holy Word is, indeed, a tool for transforming our lives, and unless we treat it that way, we suffer the bitter consequences of our shortsightedness.

Would you like to energize your marriage and your life? Then pick up your Bible and read it with a focused mind and an open heart. And remember: God has given you the Bible for the purpose of knowing His promises, His power, His commandments, His wisdom, His love, and His Son. As you and your wife study God's teachings and apply them to your life, you will live by the Word that shall never pass away.

The instrument of our sanctification is the Word of God. The Spirit of God brings to our minds the precepts and doctrines of truth, and applies them with power. The truth is our sanctifier. If we do not hear or read it, we will not grow in sanctification.

C. H. Spurgeon

God gives us a compass and a Book of promises and principles—the Bible—and lets us make our decisions day by day as we sense the leading of His Spirit. This is how we grow.

Warren Wiersbe

The Bible is the one Book to which any thoughtful man may go with any honest question of life or destiny and find the answer of God by honest searching.

John Ruskin

Man shall not live by bread alone, but by every word that proceeds from the mouth of God.

Matthew 4:4 NKJV

Today's Prayer

Dear Lord, the Bible is Your gift to our marriage, to our family, and to our world. Let us trust it and use it today and every day that we live. Amen

Too Busy?

Careful planning puts you ahead in the long run; hurry and scurry puts you further behind.

Proverbs 21:5 MSG

A re you and your wife making time each day to praise God and to study His Word? If so, you know firsthand the blessings that He offers those who worship Him consistently and sincerely. But, if you have unintentionally allowed the hustle and bustle of your busy day to come between you and your Creator, then you must slow down, take a deep breath, and rearrange your priorities.

God loved this world so much that He sent His Son to save it. And now only one real question remains for you: what will you do in response to God's love? The answer should be obvious: God must come first in your life. He is the giver of all good things, and He is the One who sent His Son so that you might have eternal life. He deserves your prayers, your obedience, your stewardship, and your love—and He deserves these things all day every day, not just on Sunday mornings.

Often our lives are strangled by things that don't ultimatley matter.

Grady Nutt

This is a day when we are so busy doing everything that we have no time to be anything. Even religiously we are so occupied with activities that we have no time to know God.

Vance Havner

We often become mentally and spiritually barren because we're so busy.

Franklin Graham

You can't go wrong when you love others. When you add up everything in the law code, the sum total is love. But make sure that you don't get so absorbed and exhausted in taking care of all your day-by-day obligations that you lose track of the time and doze off, oblivious to God.

Romans 13:10-11 MSG

Today's Prayer

Dear Lord, when the quickening pace of life leaves me with little time for my marriage or for my family or for worship or for praise, help me to reorder my priorities. And let me turn to Jesus for the peace that only He can give. Amen

Managing Change

Therefore do not worry about tomorrow, for tomorrow will worry about itself. Each day has enough trouble of its own.
Matthew 6:34 NIV

A re you and your wife facing difficult circumstances or unwelcome changes? If so, please remember that God is far bigger than any problem you may face. So, instead of worrying about life's inevitable challenges, put your faith in the Father and His only begotten Son: "Jesus Christ is the same yesterday, today, and forever" (Hebrews 13:8 NKJV). And remember: it is precisely because your Savior does not change that you can face your challenges with courage for today and hope for tomorrow.

Life is often challenging, but as Christians, we should not be afraid. God loves us, and He will protect us. In times of hardship, He will comfort us; in times of change, He will guide our steps. When we are troubled, weak, or sorrowful, God is always with us. We must build our lives on the rock that cannot be moved . . . we must trust in God. Always.

In a world kept chaotic by change, you will eventually discover, as I have, that this is one of the most precious qualities of the God we are looking for: He doesn't change.

Bill Hybels

Mere change is not growth. Growth is the synthesis of change and continuity, and where there is no continuity there is no growth.

C. S. Lewis

The resurrection of Jesus Christ is the power of God to change history and to change lives.

Bill Bright

The wise see danger ahead and avoid it, but fools keep going and get into trouble.

Proverbs 27:12 NCV

Today's Prayer

Dear Lord, our world is constantly changing. When my wife and I face the inevitable transitions of life, we will turn to You for strength and assurance. Thank You, Father, for love that is unchanging and everlasting. Amen

Day 29

Relying Upon Him

*Therefore humble yourselves under the mighty hand of God,
that He may exalt you at the proper time, casting all your
anxiety on Him, because He cares for you.*

1 Peter 5:6-7 NASB

Make no mistake about it: God is your ultimate source of security. The world offers no safety nets, but God does. He sent His only begotten Son to offer you the priceless gift of eternal life. And now you are challenged to return God's love by obeying His commandments and honoring His Son.

When you and your spouse allow Christ to reign over your lives and your marriage, you will be secure. When you and your beloved feel God's presence and invite His Son to rule your hearts and your household, your family will be eternally blessed.

In a world filled with dangers and temptations, God is the ultimate armor. In a world filled with misleading messages, God's Word is the ultimate truth. In a world filled with more frustrations than we can count, God's Son offers the ultimate peace.

Will you and your spouse accept God's peace and wear God's armor against the dangers of our world? Hopefully so—because when you do, you can live courageously, knowing that you possess the ultimate security: God's unfailing love for you.

Faith is not merely you holding on to God—it is God holding on to you.

E. Stanley Jones

The more you give your mental burdens to the Lord, the more exciting it becomes to see how God will handle things that are impossible for you to do anything about.

Charles Swindoll

He gives power to the weak, and to those who have no might He increases strength.

Isaiah 40:29 NKJV

Today's Prayer

Dear Lord, You have promised never to leave us or forsake us. You are always with my wife and I, protecting us and encouraging us. Whatever this day may bring, we thank You for Your love and for Your strength. We will lean upon You, Father, this day and forever. Amen

Genuine Contentment

The LORD gives strength to his people;
the LORD blesses his people with peace.

Psalm 29:11 NIV

Everywhere we turn, or so it seems, the world promises us contentment and happiness. But the contentment that the world offers is fleeting and incomplete. Thankfully, the contentment that God offers is all encompassing and everlasting.

Happiness depends less upon our circumstances than upon our thoughts. When we turn our thoughts to God, to His gifts, and to His glorious creation, we experience the joy that God intends for His children. But, when we focus on the negative aspects of life—or when we disobey God's commandments—we cause ourselves needless suffering.

Do you and your wife sincerely want to be contented Christians? Then set your minds and your hearts upon God's love and His grace. The fullness of life in Christ is available to all who seek it and claim it. Count yourselves among that number.

If you don't find contentment through God, you will never find it anywhere else. So, put your faith and your trust in Him. When God dwells at the center of your lives, peace and contentment will belong to you just as surely as you belong to God.

The secret of contentment in the midst of change is found in having roots in the changeless Christ—the same yesterday, today and forever.

Ed Young

God is most glorified in us when we are most satisfied in him.

John Piper

Contentment is not escape from battle, but rather an abiding peace and confidence in the midst of battle.

Warren Wiersbe

But godliness with contentment is a great gain.

1 Timothy 6:6 Holman CSB

Today's Prayer

Dear Lord, You offer us contentment and peace; let my wife and I accept Your peace. Help us to trust Your Word, to follow Your commandments, and to welcome the peace of Jesus into our hearts, today and forever. Amen

Christ's Abundance

I have come that they may have life,
and that they may have it more abundantly.
John 10:10 NKJV

Christ came in order that we might have life abundant and life eternal. Eternal life is the priceless possession of all who invite Christ into their hearts, but God's abundance is optional: He does not force it upon us.

When we entrust our hearts and our days to the One who created us, we experience abundance through the grace and sacrifice of His Son. But, when we turn our thoughts and direct our energies away from God's commandments, we inevitably forfeit the spiritual abundance that might otherwise be ours.

God intends that the institution of marriage should be a continuing source of abundance for husbands and wives alike. But it's up to husbands and wives to claim God's abundance . . . or not.

Have you and your wife accepted God's gift of abundance? If so, your marriage should reflect that decision. When you both honor God and obey Him without reservation, you will receive the love and the abundance that He has promised.

Would you like a formula for a successful marriage? Seek first the kingdom of God and encourage your wife to do likewise. Then, prepare yourselves for the joy, the peace, and the spiritual abundance that the Shepherd offers His sheep.

The only way you can experience abundant life is to surrender your plans to Him.

Charles Stanley

Jesus wants Life for us, Life with a capital L.

John Eldredge

Come to terms with God and be at peace; in this way good will come to you.

Job 22:21 Holman CSB

Today's Prayer

Heavenly Father, You have promised that my wife and I can experience abundance through Your Son Jesus. We thank You, Lord, for Your abundance. Guide us according to Your will, so that we might be worthy servants in all that we say and do, this day and every day. Amen

Let the Celebration Begin

I've told you these things for a purpose: that my joy
might be your joy, and your joy wholly mature.
John 15:11 MSG

How quick are you to celebrate your life, your marriage, and your wife? Christ made it clear to His followers: He intended that His joy would become their joy. And it still holds true today: Christ intends that His believers share His love with joy in their hearts. Yet sometimes, amid the inevitable hustle and bustle of life here on earth, we can forfeit—albeit temporarily—the joy of Christ as we wrestle with the challenges of daily living.

Joy is an important part of healthy Christian marriages. Joyful spouses tend to share their joy with each other, and that's exactly what God intends.

C. H. Spurgeon, the renowned 19th-century English clergymen, advised, "The Lord is glad to open the gate to every knocking soul. It opens very freely; its hinges are not rusted; no bolts secure it. Have faith and enter at this moment through holy courage. If you knock with a heavy heart, you shall yet sing with joy of spirit. Never be discouraged!"

Are you doing your best to live each day as a joyful servant of Christ? And, are you inviting your wife to join in the celebration? Hopefully so. After all, few things in life are more wonderful to behold than the joining together of two joyful believers. So now, with no further ado, thank God for your marriage, and let the celebration begin!

When Jesus Christ is the source of our joy, no words can describe it.

Billy Graham

Joy is the serious business of heaven.

C. S. Lewis

Rejoice, and be exceeding glad: for great is your reward in heaven . . . .

Matthew 5:12 KJV

Today's Prayer

Dear Lord, You have given us so many blessings. Make us thankful, loving, responsible, and wise. My wife and I praise You, Father, for the gift of Your Son and for the priceless gift of salvation. Make us joyful Christians, make us worthy examples to others, and make us dutiful servants to You, now and forever. Amen

Treasure the Time You Spend Together

Enjoy life with the wife you love all the days of your fleeting life, which has been given to you under the sun, all your fleeting days.

Ecclesiastes 9:9 Holman CSB

It takes time to build a strong marriage . . . lots of time. Yet we live in a world where time seems to be an ever-shrinking commodity as we rush from place to place with seldom a moment to spare.

Has the busy pace of life robbed you of high quality time with your bride? If so, it's time to adjust your priorities. And God can help.

When you fervently ask God to help you prioritize your life, He will give you guidance. When you seek His guidance every day, your Creator will reveal Himself in a variety of ways. As a follower of Christ, you must do no less.

When you allow God to help you organize your day, you'll soon discover that there is ample time for your spouse and your family. When you make God a full partner in every aspect of your life, He will lead you along the proper path: His path. When you allow God to reign over your heart, He will honor you with spiritual blessings that are simply too numerous to count. So, as you plan for the day ahead, make God's priorities your priorities. When you do, every other priority will have a tendency to fall neatly into place.

A marriage can't survive forever on leftovers. It needs to be fed continually, or it will eventually starve.

John Maxwell

Sin is largely a matter of mistaken priorities. Any sin in us that is cherished, hidden, and not confessed will cut the nerve center of our faith.

Catherine Marshall

Don't abandon wisdom, and she will watch over you; love her, and she will guard you.

Proverbs 4:6 Holman CSB

Today's Prayer

Dear Lord, let Your priorities be our priorities. Let Your will be our will. Let Your Word be our guide, and let us grow in faith and in wisdom this day and every day. Amen

Day 34

Infinite Possibilities

Is anything too hard for the LORD?
Genesis 18:14 KJV

A re you and your wife afraid to ask God to do big things? Is your faith threadbare and worn? If so, it's time to abandon your doubts and reclaim your faith in God's promises.

Ours is a God of infinite possibilities. But sometimes, because of limited faith and limited understanding, we wrongly assume that God cannot or will not intervene in the affairs of mankind. Such assumptions are simply wrong.

God's Holy Word makes it clear: absolutely nothing is impossible for the Lord. And since the Bible means what it says, you can be comforted in the knowledge that the Creator of the universe can do miraculous things in your own life and in the lives of your loved ones. Your challenge, as a believer, is to take God at His word, and to expect the miraculous.

If we take God's program, we can have God's power—not otherwise.

E. Stanley Jones

You can believe in the Holy Spirit not because you see Him, but because you see what He does in people's lives when they are surrendered to Christ and possess His power.

Billy Graham

The task ahead of us is never as great as the Power behind us.

Quips, Anonymous

God is the silent partner in all great enterprises.

Abraham Lincoln

But as it is written: "Eye has not seen, nor ear heard, nor have entered into the heart of man the things which God has prepared for those who love Him."

1 Corinthians 2:9 NKJV

Today's Prayer

Dear God, nothing is impossible for You—keep us always mindful of Your strength. When we lose hope, give us faith; when others lose hope, let us tell them of Your glory and Your works. Today, Lord, let us expect the miraculous, and let us trust in You. Amen

Day 35

Giving More

A new commandment I give to you, that you love one another; as I have loved you, that you also love one another.

John 13:34 NKJV

When you're trying to figure out what to do with your free time, it's easy to think selfishly. But it's wrong. If you consistently place your own needs above the needs of your wife, you're probably headed for trouble, and fast.

Too many marriages become unbalanced when one partner assumes the role of the "taker" while the other partner accepts the role of the "giver." But the healthiest marriages are those in which both parties seek to give more than they get.

Jesus taught that the most esteemed men and women are not those who say "me first." Christ instructed us that the greatest among us will be "servants of all" (Mark 9:35). And these words are especially true in the context of marriage.

Are you willing to contribute unselfishly to the well-being of your loved ones? And are you willing to do so without constantly comparing your own good deeds to the deeds of your wife? If so, your marriage will be blessed by your unselfishness. If not, it's time to heed this word of advice: The best way to make love last is by saying "you first"—and meaning it.

Love is an attribute of God. To love others is evidence of a genuine faith.

Kay Arthur

There is no more lovely, friendly, and charming relationship, communion, or company than a good marriage.

Martin Luther

Honor all people. Love the brotherhood. Fear God. Honor the king.

1 Peter 2:17 NKJV

Today's Prayer

Dear Lord, let me treat my wife as I wish to be treated. Because I expect to receive kindness, let me be kind. Because I wish to be loved, let me be loving. Because I need forgiveness, let me be merciful. In all things, Lord, let us live by the Golden Rule, and let me teach that rule to others through my words and my deeds. Amen

The Media's Messages

*Let no one deceive himself. If anyone among you seems to
be wise in this age, let him become a fool that he may become
wise. For the wisdom of this world is foolishness
with God. For it is written, "He catches the wise
in their own craftiness."*
1 Corinthians 3:18–19 NKJV

I f you and your wife have acquired the bad habit of
watching whatever happens to pop up on your family's
TV screen, it's time to rethink the way you control
your clicker. Most television networks (as well as the
other forms of popular media) can be dangerous to your
emotional and spiritual health.

The media is working around the clock in an attempt to
rearrange your family's priorities in ways that are definitely
not in your best interests. The media is trying to teach
your family that physical appearance is all-important, that
material possessions should be acquired at any cost, and
that the world operates independently of God's laws. But
guess what? Those messages are lies.

In the pursuit of profits, the media glamorizes violence,
exploits suffering, and sensationalizes sex, all in the name
of "ratings" (translated: "money").

So here's a question for you and your family: Will you control what appears on your TV screen, or will you be controlled by it? If you're willing to take complete control over the images that appear inside the four walls of your home, you'll be doing yourselves a king-sized favor. So forget the media hype, and pay attention to God. Stand up for Him and be counted, not just in church where it's relatively easy to be a Christian, but also when you're deciding what to watch. You owe it to your Creator . . . and you owe it to yourselves.

The popular media has a way of attacking your senses and your heart. Approach the media with care.

Criswell Freeman

Do not love the world or the things in the world. If anyone loves the world, the love of the Father is not in him.

1 John 2:15 NKJV

Today's Prayer

Lord, this world is filled with temptations and distractions; we have many opportunities to stray from Your commandments. Help us to focus, not on the things of this world, but on the message of Your Son. Let us keep Christ in our hearts as we follow Him this day and forever. Amen

A Man of Faith

For whatever is born of God overcomes the world.
And this is the victory that has overcome
the world—our faith.

1 John 5:4 NKJV

W̶ould you and your wife like to strengthen the bonds of your marriage? Here's a wonderful place to start: by strengthening your faith in God.

Every life and every marriage is a series of successes and failures, celebrations and disappointments, joys and sorrows. Every step of the way, through every triumph and tragedy, God will stand by your side and strengthen you . . . if you have faith in Him. Jesus taught His disciples that if they had faith, they could move mountains. You can too.

When a suffering woman sought healing by merely touching the hem of His cloak, Jesus replied, "Daughter, be of good comfort; thy faith hath made thee whole" (Matthew 9:22 KJV). The message to believers of every generation is clear: we must live by faith today and every day.

When you and your wife place your faith, your trust, indeed your life in the hands of Christ Jesus, you'll be amazed at the marvelous things He can do with you and through you. So strengthen your faith and your marriage through praise, through worship, through Bible study, and through prayer. And trust God's plans. With Him, all things are possible, and He stands ready to open a world of possibilities to you and yours . . . if you have faith.

The Christian life is one of faith, where we find ourselves routinely overdriving our headlights but knowing it's okay because God is in control and has a purpose behind it.

Bill Hybels

Faith, as Paul saw it, was a living, flaming thing leading to surrender and obedience to the commandments of Christ.

A. W. Tozer

Now without faith it is impossible to please God, for the one who draws near to Him must believe that He exists and rewards those who seek Him.

Hebrews 11:6 Holman CSB

Today's Prayer

Dear Lord, keep my wife and me mindful that You are always near and that You can overcome any challenge. With Your love and Your power, Father, we can live courageously and faithfully today and every day. Amen

Day 38

Forgive: It's God's Way

Be kind to one another, tender-hearted, forgiving each other, just as God in Christ also has forgiven you.

Ephesians 4:32 NASB

If you want to make your love last a lifetime, you and your wife we must learn the art of forgiveness. Why? Because all of our loved ones are imperfect (as are we). How often must we forgive each other? More times than we can count. In other words, we must not just learn how to forgive; we must learn how to keep forgiving (Matthew 18:21-22).

Perhaps granting forgiveness is hard for you. If so, you are not alone. Granting heartfelt forgiveness is often difficult for hardheaded husbands—difficult but not impossible.

When it comes to the hard work of forgiving those who have injured us, God is willing to help, but He expects us to do some of the work—and when we do so, we are blessed.

When we learn the art of forgiveness, we earn peace within our marriages and peace within our hearts. But when we harbor bitterness against others, we forfeit that peace—and by doing so, we bring needless harm to ourselves and to our loved ones. So, if there exists even one person, alive or dead, whom you have not forgiven (and that includes yourself or your wife), follow God's commandment—forgive. Because bitterness, anger, and regret are emotions that have no place in your life or your marriage.

Our forgiveness toward others should flow from a realization and appreciation of God's forgiveness toward us.

Franklin Graham

Forgiveness is God's command.

Martin Luther

A person's insight gives him patience, and his virtue is to overlook an offense.

Proverbs 19:11 Holman CSB

Today's Prayer

Dear Lord, You command us to forgive each other quickly, thoroughly, and often. Keep us mindful, Father, that we are never fully liberated until we have been freed from the chains of anger—and that You offer us that freedom through Your Son Jesus. Amen

Day 39

Choosing Wisely

*If you need wisdom—if you want to know what God
wants you to do—ask him, and he will gladly tell you.
He will not resent your asking.*

James 1:5 NLT

Because we are creatures of free will, we make
choices—lots of them. When we make choices
that are pleasing to our Heavenly Father, we are
blessed. When we make choices that cause us to walk in
the footsteps of God's Son, we feel better about ourselves
and we enjoy the abundance that Christ has promised to
those who follow Him. But when we make choices that are
displeasing to God, we sow seeds that have the potential
to bring forth a bitter harvest.

Today, as you and your wife encounter the challenges
of everyday living, you will make hundreds of choices.
And it's up to both of you to choose wisely. So today and
every day, make your thoughts and your actions pleasing
to God. And remember: every choice that is displeasing to
Him is the wrong choice—no exceptions.

We are either the masters or the victims of our attitudes. It is a matter of personal choice. Who we are today is the result of choices we made yesterday. Tomorrow, we will become what we choose today. To change means to choose to change.

John Maxwell

Good and evil both increase at compound interest. That is why the little decisions you and I make every day are of such infinite importance.

C. S. Lewis

Life is a series of choices between the bad, the good, and the best. Everything depends on how we choose.

Vance Havner

But the wisdom that is from above is first pure, then peaceable, gentle, willing to yield, full of mercy and good fruits, without partiality and without hypocrisy.

James 3:17 NKJV

Today's Prayer

Dear Lord, today I will focus my thoughts on Your will for my life. I will strive to make decisions that are pleasing to You, and I will care for my wife and family as I follow in the footsteps of Your Son. Amen

Courtesy Matters

Dear friend, you are showing your faith by whatever you do
for the brothers, and this you are doing for strangers.

3 John 1:5 Holman CSB

id Christ instruct us in matters of etiquette and courtesy? Of course He did. Christ's instructions are clear: "In everything, therefore, treat people the same way you want them to treat you, for this is the Law and the Prophets" (Matthew 7:12 NASB). Jesus did not say, "In some things, treat people as you wish to be treated." And, He did not say, "From time to time, treat others with kindness." Christ said that we should treat others as we wish to be treated in every aspect of our daily lives. This, of course, is a tall order indeed, but as Christians, we are commanded to do our best.

Today, be a little kinder than necessary to your wife, to family members, to friends, and to total strangers. And, as you consider all the things that Christ has done in your life, honor Him with your words and with your deeds. He expects no less, and He deserves no less.

Only the courteous can love, but it is love that makes them courteous.

C. S. Lewis

You will accomplish more by kind words and a courteous manner than by anger and sharp rebuke, which should never be used, except in necessity.

St. Angela Merici

Courtesy is contagious.

Marie T. Freeman

When you extend hospitality to others, you're not trying to impress people; you're trying to reflect God to them.

Max Lucado

Don't neglect to show hospitality, for by doing this some have welcomed angels as guests without knowing it.

Hebrews 13:2 Holman CSB

Today's Prayer

Help us, Lord, to treat everyone—especially each other—with courtesy and respect. You have created each person in Your own image; we are all Your children, Father. So let us show kindness to all. Amen

Day 41

Be Still

Be silent before the Lord and wait expectantly for Him.
Psalm 37:7 Holman CSB

Silence is, indeed, golden—and like gold, it's a scarce commodity. Ours is a noisy, fast-paced world. The demands of the day can seem overwhelming at times, but when we slow ourselves down and seek the presence of a loving God, we invite His peace into our hearts.

Do you and your wife carve out quiet moments each day to offer thanksgiving and praise to your Creator? You should. During these moments of stillness, you will often sense the infinite love and power of our Lord.

The familiar words of Psalm 46:10 remind us to "Be still, and know that I am God." When we do so, we encounter the awesome presence of our loving Heavenly Father, and we are blessed beyond words.

We can seek God and find him! God is knowable, touchable, hearable, seeable, with the mind, the hands, the ears, and eyes of the inner man.

A. W. Tozer

Let your loneliness be transformed into a holy aloneness. Sit still before the Lord. Remember Naomi's word to Ruth: "Sit still, my daughter, until you see how the matter will fall."

Elisabeth Elliot

I suggest you discipline yourself to spend time daily in a systematic reading of God's Word. Make this "quiet time" a priority that nobody can change.

Warren Wiersbe

In quietness and confidence shall be your strength.

Isaiah 30:15 NKJV

Today's Prayer

Dear Lord, let us be still before You. When we are hurried or distracted, slow us down and redirect our thoughts. When we are confused, give us perspective. Keep us mindful, Father, that You are always with us. And let us sense Your presence now and forever. Amen

Day 42

Ignoring Sin

For everyone who practices wicked things hates the light and avoids it, so that his deeds may not be exposed. But anyone who lives by the truth comes to the light, so that his works may be shown to be accomplished by God.

John 3:20–21 Holman CSB

I f we deny our sins, we allow those sins to flourish. And if we allow sinful behaviors to become habits, we invite hardships into our own lives and into the lives of our loved ones. When we yield to the distractions and temptations of this troubled world, we suffer. But God has other intentions, and His plans for our lives do not include sin or denial.

When we allow ourselves to encounter God's presence, He will lead us away from temptation, away from confusion, and away from the self-deception. God is the champion of truth and the enemy of denial. May we see ourselves through His eyes and conduct ourselves accordingly.

Unconfessed sin in your life will cause you to doubt.

Anne Graham Lotz

What I like about experience is that it is such an honest thing. You may take any number of wrong turnings; but keep your eyes open and you will not be allowed to go very far before the warning signs appear. You may have deceived yourself, but experience is not trying to deceive you. The universe rings true wherever you fairly test it.

C. S. Lewis

We cannot out-sin God's ability to forgive us.

Beth Moore

Disaster pursues sinners, but good rewards the righteous.

Proverbs 13:21 Holman CSB

Today's Prayer

Dear Lord, when I displease You, I do injury to myself, to my family, and to my community. Because sin distances me from You, Lord, I will fear sin and I will avoid sinful places. The fear of sinning against You is a healthy fear, Father, because it can motivate me to accomplish Your will. Let a healthy fear of sin guide my path, today and every day of my life. Amen

Give Me Patience, Lord, Right Now!

Love is patient; love is kind.

1 Corinthians 13:4 Holman CSB

Marriage is an exercise in patience. From time to time, even if your wife is the most considerate woman in the world, she may do things that confound you, confuse you, or anger you. Why? Because even the most considerate woman in the world is still an imperfect human being, capable of missteps, misdeeds, and mistakes. So, because your bride is a fallible-yet-lovable woman, you should learn to be patient with her shortcomings (just as she, too, must be patient with yours).

Are you one of those guys who demand perfection from everybody, with the possible exception of yourself? If so, it's time to reassess your expectations. God doesn't expect perfection, and neither should you.

Proverbs 19:11 makes it clear: "People with good sense restrain their anger; they earn esteem by overlooking wrongs" (NLT). So the next time you find yourself drumming your fingers while waiting for your wife to do the right thing, take a deep breath and ask God for patience. After all, the world unfolds according to God's timetable, not yours. And your loved ones live—and grow—according to their own timetables, too. Sometimes, you must wait patiently, and that's as it should be. After all, think how patient God has been with you.

The next time you're disappointed, don't panic. Don't give up. Just be patient and let God remind you he's still in control.

Max Lucado

Two signposts of faith: "Slow Down" and "Wait Here."

Charles Stanley

We urge you, brethren, admonish the unruly, encourage the fainthearted, help the weak, be patient with everyone.

1 Thessalonians 5:14 NASB

Today's Prayer

Heavenly Father, give us patience. Let us live according to Your plan and according to Your timetable. When we are hurried, slow us down. When we become impatient with others, give us empathy. When we are frustrated by the demands of the day, give us peace. Today, let us be patient Christians, Dear Lord, as we trust in You and in Your master plan for our lives. Amen

Making Peace with Your Past

The Lord says, "Forget what happened before, and do not think about the past. Look at the new thing I am going to do. It is already happening. Don't you see it? I will make a road in the desert and rivers in the dry land."

Isaiah 43:18-19 NCV

Because you are human, you may be slow to forget yesterday's disappointments. But, if you sincerely seek to focus your hopes and energies on the future, then you must find ways to accept the past, no matter how difficult it may be to do so.

Have you and your wife made peace with the past? If so, congratulations. But, if you are mired in the quicksand of regret, it's time to plan your escape. How can you do so? By accepting what has been and by trusting God for what will be.

So, if you have not yet made peace with the past, today is the day to declare an end to all hostilities. When you do, you can then turn your thoughts to the wondrous promises of God and to the glorious future that He has in store for you and your wife.

The wise man gives proper appreciation in his life to his past. He learns to sift the sawdust of heritage in order to find the nuggets that make the current moment have any meaning.

Grady Nutt

The wise and diligent traveler watches his every step, and always has his eyes upon the part of the road directly in front of him. But he does not turn constantly backward to count every step, and to examine every track. He would lose time in going forward.

François Fènelon

I do not consider myself yet to have taken hold of it. But one thing I do: Forgetting what is behind and straining toward what is ahead, I press on toward the goal to win the prize for which God has called me heavenward in Christ Jesus.

Philippians 3:13-14 NIV

Today's Prayer

Heavenly Father, when we are bitter, we cannot experience Your peace. So free us from anger, resentment, and envy. Keep us mindful, Lord, that forgiveness is Your commandment, and help us accept the past, treasure the present, and trust the future . . . to You. Amen

Honoring God

Honor GOD with everything you own;
give him the first and the best.
Your barns will burst, your wine vats will brim over.

Proverbs 3:9-10 MSG

Whom will you and your wife choose to honor today? If you honor God and place Him at the center of your marriage, every day is a cause for celebration.

When we honor God and place Him at the center of our lives, every day is a cause for celebration. God fills each day to the brim with possibilities, and He challenges us to use our lives for His purposes. Every morning at dawn, the sun breaks over God's glorious creation. The new day is presented to us free of charge, but we must beware: Today is a non-renewable resource—once it's gone, it's gone forever. Our responsibility is to use this day in the service of God's will and in the service of His people.

God shows unbridled delight when He sees people acting in ways that honor Him.

Bill Hybels

We honor God by asking for great things when they are a part of His promise. We dishonor Him and cheat ourselves when we ask for molehills where He has promised mountains.

Vance Havner

What lessons about honor did you learn from your childhood? Are you living what you learned today?

Dennis Swanberg

Enter into His gates with thanksgiving, and into His courts with praise. Be thankful to Him, and bless His name. For the Lord is good; His mercy is everlasting, and His truth endures to all generations.

Psalm 100:4-5 NKJV

Today's Prayer

I praise You, Lord, from the depths of my heart, and I give thanks for Your goodness, for Your mercy, and for Your Son. Let me honor You every day of my life through my words and my deeds. Let me honor You, Father, with all that I am. Amen

The Voice Inside Your Head

*So I strive always to keep my conscience clear
before God and man.*
Acts 24:16 NIV

Your conscience is an early-warning system designed to keep you out of trouble. When you're about to do something that you know is wrong, a little voice inside your head has a way of speaking up. If you listen to that voice, you'll be okay; if you ignore it, you're asking for headaches, heartbreaks, or both.

Whenever you're about to make an important decision, you should listen carefully to the quiet voice inside. Sometimes, of course, it's tempting to do otherwise. From time to time you'll be tempted to abandon your better judgement by ignoring your conscience. But remember: a conscience is a terrible thing to waste. So instead of ignoring that quiet little voice, pay careful attention to it. If you do, your conscience will lead you in the right direction—in fact, it's trying to lead you right now. So listen . . . and learn.

You should not believe your conscience and your feelings more than the word which the Lord who receives sinners preaches to you.

Martin Luther

The voice of the subconscious argues with you, tries to convince you; but the inner voice of God does not argue; it does not try to convince you. It just speaks, and it is self-authenticating.

E. Stanley Jones

The beginning of backsliding means your conscience does not answer to the truth.

Oswald Sanders

Let us draw near with a true heart in full assurance of faith, our hearts sprinkled clean from an evil conscience and our bodies washed in pure water.

Hebrews 10:22 Holman CSB

Today's Prayer

Dear God, You've given me a conscience that tells me right from wrong. Let me trust my conscience, and let me live according to Your teachings, not just for today, but forever. Amen

Your Real Riches

*Don't collect for yourselves treasures on earth, where moth
and rust destroy and where thieves break in and steal. But
collect for yourselves treasures in heaven, where neither moth
nor rust destroys, and where thieves don't break in and steal.
For where your treasure is, there your heart will be also.*

Matthew 6:19-21 Holman CSB

Earthly riches are temporary. Spiritual riches, on the other hand, are everlasting. Yet all too often, we focus our thoughts and energies on the accumulation of earthly treasures, leaving precious little time for anything else.

Far too many marriages are weighted down by endless concerns about money and possessions. Too many couples mistakenly focus their thoughts and efforts on newer cars, better clothes, and bigger houses. The results of these misplaced priorities are always unfortunate, and sometimes tragic.

Certainly we all need the basic necessities of life, but once we meet those needs for our families and ourselves, the piling up of possessions creates more problems than it solves. Our real riches are not of this world: we are never really rich until we are rich in spirit.

Do you find yourself wrapped up in the concerns of the material world? If so, it's time for you and your wife to sit down and have a heart-to-heart talk about "stuff." When you do, you should reorder your priorities by turning away from materialism and back to God. Then, you can begin storing up riches that will endure throughout eternity: the spiritual kind.

What we possess often possesses us—we are possessed by possessions.

Oswald Chambers

He said, "I came naked from my mother's womb, and I will be stripped of everything when I die. The LORD gave me everything I had, and the LORD has taken it away. Praise the name of the LORD!"

Job 1:21 NLT

Today's Prayer

Lord, our greatest possession is our relationship with You through Jesus Christ. You have promised that, when we first seek Your kingdom and Your righteousness, You will give us the things we need. We will trust You completely, Lord, for our needs, both material and spiritual, this day and always. Amen

Day 48

A Foundation of Trust

Honor marriage, and guard the sacredness of
sexual intimacy between wife and husband.
God draws a firm line against casual and illicit sex.
Hebrews 13:4 MSG

The best relationships—and the best marriages—
are built upon a foundation of honesty and trust.
Without trust, marriages soon begin to wither;
with trust, marriages soon begin to flourish.

For Christian men and women, honesty is the right
policy because it's God's policy. God's Word makes it clear:
"Lying lips are an abomination to the Lord, but those who
deal truthfully are His delight" (Proverbs 12:22 NKJV).

Sometimes, honesty is difficult; sometimes, honesty is
painful; sometimes, honesty makes us feel uncomfortable.
Despite these temporary feelings of discomfort, we must
make honesty the hallmark of all our relationships;
otherwise, we invite needless suffering into our own lives
and into the lives of those we love.

Do you want your love to last forever? Then you and
your wife must build a marriage based upon mutual trust
and unerring truth. Both of you deserve nothing less . . .
and neither, for that matter, does God.

Truth becomes hard if it is not softened by love, and love becomes soft if not strengthened by truth.

E. Stanley Jones

My commitment to my marriage vows places me in an utterly unique and profoundly significant relationship with the most important human being on earth—my spouse.

Joni Eareckson Tada

A lie is like a snowball: the further you roll it, the bigger it becomes.

Martin Luther

Trust is like "money in the bank" in a marriage. There must be a reasonable amount of it on deposit to ensure the security of a marital union.

Ed Young

The one who lives with integrity lives securely, but whoever perverts his ways will be found out.

Proverbs 10:9 Holman CSB

Today's Prayer

Dear Lord, You instruct me to walk in truth. Give me the courage to behave honorably, to speak honestly, and to walk faithfully with Your Son today and every day. Amen

Conquering Everyday Frustrations

A hot-tempered man stirs up dissention,
but a patient man calms a quarrel.
Proverbs 15:18 NIV

Anger is a natural human emotion that is sometimes necessary and appropriate. Even Jesus became angry when confronted with the moneychangers in the temple (Matthew 21:12). Righteous indignation is an appropriate response to evil, but God does not intend that anger should rule our lives. And, just as importantly, God does not intend that anger should rule our marriages. He instructs us to turn away from anger whenever possible and forgive others just as we seek forgiveness for ourselves. And forgiveness, like so many other things, starts at home.

Life is full of frustrations: some great and some small. Most of our frustrations are of the more mundane variety. As long as we live, we will inevitably face countless opportunities to lose our tempers over small, relatively insignificant events: a traffic jam, a spilled cup of coffee, an inconsiderate comment, a forgotten promise.

When you are tempted to lose your temper over the

minor inconveniences of life, don't. And while you're at it, don't bring anger into the sanctity of your marriage. Turn away from anger and turn instead to God. When you do, you'll honor Him by sharing His gift: the gift of peace. And what a beautiful gift it is.

When you strike out in anger, you may miss the other person, but you will always hit yourself.

Jim Gallery

Take no action in a furious passion. It's putting to sea in a storm.

Thomas Fuller

A patient man has great understanding, but a quick-tempered man displays folly.

Proverbs 14:29 NIV

Today's Prayer

Lord, sometimes, in moments of frustration, we become angry. When my wife and I fall prey to irrational anger, give us inner calm. Let us show our thankfulness to You by offering forgiveness to each other. And, when we do, let others see Your love reflected through our words and our deeds. Amen

Becoming Wise

He who walks with the wise grows wise . . . .
Proverbs 13:20 NIV

Sometimes, amid the concerns of everyday life, we lose perspective. Life seems out of balance as we confront an array of demands that sap our strength and cloud our thoughts. What's needed is a renewed faith, a fresh perspective, and God's wisdom.

Here in the 21st century, commentary is commonplace and information is everywhere. But the ultimate source of wisdom, the kind of timeless wisdom that God willingly shares with His children, is still available from a single unique source: the Holy Bible.

The wisdom of the world changes with the ever-shifting sands of public opinion. God's wisdom does not. His wisdom is eternal. It never changes. And it most certainly is the wisdom that you must use to plan your day, your life, and your eternal destiny.

Wisdom is the foundation, and justice is the work without which a foundation cannot stand.

St. Ambrose

The theme of Proverbs is wisdom, the right use of knowledge. It enables you to evaluate circumstances and people and make the right decisions in life.

Warren Wiersbe

Indeed, wisdom and discernment are among the natural results of a prayer-filled life.

Richard Foster

The more wisdom enters our hearts, the more we will be able to trust our hearts in difficult situations.

John Eldredge

Those who are wise will shine as bright as the sky, and those who turn many to righteousness will shine like stars forever.

Daniel 12:3 NLT

Today's Prayer

We seek wisdom, Lord, not as the world gives, but as You give. Lead us in Your ways and teach us from Your Word so that, in time, our wisdom might glorify Your kingdom and Your Son. Amen

God's Timetable

Humble yourselves, therefore, under God's mighty hand,
that he may lift you up in due time.
1 Peter 5:6 NIV

Sometimes, the hardest thing to do is to wait. This is especially true when we're in a hurry and when we want things to happen now, if not sooner! But God's plan does not always happen in the way that we would like or at the time of our own choosing. Our task—as thoughtful men and women who trust in a benevolent, all-knowing Father—is to wait patiently for God to reveal Himself.

We humans know precisely what we want, and we know exactly when we want it. But, God has a far better plan for each of us. He has created a world that unfolds according to His own timetable, not ours . . . thank goodness! And if we're wise, we trust Him and we wait patiently for Him. After all, He is trustworthy, and He always knows best.

Events of all sorts creep or fly exactly as God pleases.

William Cowper

Will not the Lord's time be better than your time?

C. H. Spurgeon

God is not hurried along in the Time-stream of this universe any more than an author is hurried along in the imaginary time of his own novel. He has infinite attention to spare for each one of us. He does not have to deal with us in the mass. You are as much alone with Him as if you were the only being He had ever created. When Christ died, He died for you individually just as much as if you have been the only man in the world.

C. S. Lewis

Wait for the LORD; be strong and take heart and wait for the LORD.

Psalm 27:14 NIV

Today's Prayer

Dear Lord, Your timing is always right for my wife and for me. You have plans for us that are grander than we can imagine. When we are impatient, remind us that You are never early or late. You are always on time, Father, so let us trust in You . . . always. Amen

Christ's Love Changes Everything

Who can separate us from the love of Christ? Can affliction or anguish or persecution or famine or nakedness or danger or sword? . . . No, in all these things we are more than victorious through Him who loved us.

Romans 8:35,37 Holman CSB

Christ's love is perfect and steadfast. Even though we are fallible, and wayward, the Good Shepherd cares for us still. What does the love of Christ mean to His believers? It changes everything. Even though we have fallen far short of the Father's commandments, Christ loves us with a power and depth that is beyond our understanding. And, as we accept Christ's love and walk in Christ's footsteps, our lives bear testimony to His power and to His grace. Yes, Christ's love changes everything; may we invite Him into our hearts so it can then change everything in us.

Christ is the ultimate Savior of mankind and the personal Savior of those who believe in Him. As His servants, we should place Him at the very center of our lives. And, every day that God gives us breath, we should share Christ's love and His message with a world that needs both.

Paul made it clear that we can never be separated from the love of Christ. This message has provided comfort to believers of every generation . . . and it should provide comfort to you and your loved ones.

There is not a single thing that Jesus cannot change, control, and conquer because He is the living Lord.

Franklin Graham

He loved us not because we're lovable, but because He is love.

C. S. Lewis

Your old life is dead. Your new life, which is your real life—even though invisible to spectators—is with Christ in God. He is your life.

Colossians 3:3 MSG

Today's Prayer

Dear Jesus, You are our Savior and our Protector. Give us the courage to trust You completely. Today, my wife and I will praise You, we will honor You, and we will live according to Your commandments, so that through us, others might come to know Your perfect love. Amen

Demonstrating Your Beliefs

Walk in a manner worthy of the God who calls you into His own kingdom and glory.

1 Thessalonians 2:12 NASB

As a Christian husband, you must do your best to make sure that your actions are accurate reflections of your beliefs. Your theology must be demonstrated, not only by your words but, more importantly, by your actions. In short, you should be a practical believer, quick to act whenever you see an opportunity to serve God.

English clergyman Thomas Fuller observed, "He does not believe who does not live according to his beliefs." These words are most certainly true. We may proclaim our beliefs to our hearts' content, but our proclamations will mean nothing—to others or to ourselves—unless we accompany our words with deeds that match. The sermons that we live are far more compelling than the ones we preach.

Like it or not, your life is an accurate reflection of your creed. And so is your marriage. If these facts give you cause for concern, don't bother talking about the changes that you intend to make—make them. And then, when your good deeds speak for themselves—as they most certainly will—don't interrupt.

The temptation of the age is to look good without being good.

Brennan Manning

The best evidence of our having the truth is our walking in the truth.

Matthew Henry

By this we know that we have come to know Him, if we keep His commandments.

1 John 2:3 NASB

Today's Prayer

Dear Lord, let my words and actions show my family the changes that You have made in my life. You sent Your Son so that we might have abundant life and eternal life. Thank You, Father, for our Savior, Christ Jesus. May we follow Him, honor Him, and share His Good News, this day and every day. Amen

A Wife of Noble Character

A wife of noble character who can find?
She is worth far more than rubies.

Proverbs 31:10 NIV

Proverbs 31:10 reminds thoughtful husbands (like you) that a wife of noble character is a blessing from God, a priceless gift from above, a treasure that should be valued and protected.

Of course you already know how deeply you value your bride, but do you communicate your gratitude with words every day? And do you demonstrate your gratitude with courtesy and kindness seven days a week? If you sincerely want to be a wise husband, and a good one, that's precisely what you'll do.

A woman of strong character should be esteemed, especially in today's troubled society. After all, she inhabits a world where temptations and distractions are everywhere, or so it seems. Yet noble women, women like your wife, remain loyal and steadfast.

So today and every day, give your thanks and admiration to that good woman with whom you share your life and your marriage. She is, indeed, priceless. She is worthy of your praise.

Integrity is a sign of maturity.

Charles Swindoll

Maintaining your integrity in a world of sham is no small accomplishment.

Wayne Oates

Integrity is the glue that holds our way of life together. We must constantly strive to keep our integrity intact. When wealth is lost, nothing is lost; when health is lost, something is lost; when character is lost, all is lost.

Billy Graham

God never called us to naïveté. He called us to integrity. The biblical concept of integrity emphasizes mature innocence not childlike ignorance.

Beth Moore

In all things showing yourself to be a pattern of good works; in doctrine showing integrity, reverence, incorruptibility . . . .

Titus 2:7 NKJV

Today's Prayer

Lord, I thank You for my wife; she is a woman of noble character. My wife deserves a husband who is a man of integrity. Let me be such a man, Lord, and let my words and deeds be a testimony to You, today and always. Amen

Cheerfulness 101

A joyful heart makes a face cheerful.
Proverbs 15:13 Holman CSB

Cheerfulness is a gift that we give to others and to ourselves. And, as believers who have been saved by a risen Christ, why shouldn't we be cheerful? The answer, of course, is that we have every reason to honor our Savior with joy in our hearts, smiles on our faces, and words of celebration on our lips.

Few things in life are more sad, or, for that matter, more absurd, than grumpy Christians. Christ promises us lives of abundance and joy if we accept His love and His grace. Yet sometimes, even the most righteous among us are beset by fits of ill temper and frustration. During these moments, we may not feel like turning our thoughts and prayers to Christ, but if we seek to gain perspective and peace, that's precisely what we must do.

Are you and your wife cheerful Christians? You should be! And what is the best way to attain the joy that is rightfully yours? By giving Christ what is rightfully His: your heart, your soul, and your life.

Christ can put a spring in your step and a thrill in your heart. Optimism and cheerfulness are products of knowing Christ.

Billy Graham

It is not fitting, when one is in God's service, to have a gloomy face or a chilling look.

St. Francis of Assisi

Hope is the power of being cheerful in circumstances which we know to be desperate.

G. K. Chesterton

Be assured, my dear friend, that it is no joy to God in seeing you with a dreary countenance.

C. H. Spurgeon

Worry is a heavy load, but a kind word cheers you up.

Proverbs 12:25 NCV

Today's Prayer

Dear Lord, You have given me so many reasons to be happy. I want to be a cheerful Christian and a grateful husband. Today and every day, let me share my happiness with my wife, with my family, with my friends, and with the world. Amen

Let God Decide

Now if any of you lacks wisdom, he should ask God,
who gives to all generously and without criticizing,
and it will be given to him. But let him ask in faith
without doubting. For the doubter is like the surging sea,
driven and tossed by the wind.

James 1:5-6 Holman CSB

Decisions, decisions, decisions: every day is filled with them. And when it comes to making those decisions, this much is clear: the quality of your decisions will, to a great extent, determine the quality of your life and your marriage.

Each day, we make countless choices that can bring us closer to God and to our loved ones . . . or not. When we live according to God's commandments, we earn for ourselves the abundance and peace that He intends for our lives. But, when we turn our backs upon God by disobeying Him, we bring needless suffering upon ourselves and upon our families.

Do you seek spiritual abundance that can be yours through the person of God's only begotten Son? Then you must make right decisions, starting with the decision to invite Christ to reign over your actions and your marriage. When you do, you will receive untold blessings for yourself and for your loved ones—blessings for this day, and blessings for all eternity.

God always gives His best to those who leave the choice with Him.

Jim Elliot

I don't doubt that the Holy Spirit guides your decisions from within when you make them with the intention of pleasing God. The error would be to think that He speaks only within, whereas in reality He speaks also through Scripture, the Church, Christian friends, and books.

C. S. Lewis

But seek first the kingdom of God and His righteousness, and all these things will be provided for you.

Matthew 6:33 Holman CSB

Today's Prayer

Lord, help me to make decisions that are pleasing to You. Help me to be honest, patient, thoughtful, and obedient. And above all, help me to follow the teachings of Jesus, not just today, but every day. Amen

The Art of Cooperation

If a kingdom is divided against itself,
that kingdom cannot stand. If a house is divided against itself,
that house cannot stand.

Mark 3:24-25 Holman CSB

Have you and your wife learned the fine art of cooperation? And do you tell your wife every day that you're ready, willing, and able to help her get things done? If so, you have learned the wisdom of "give and take," not the foolishness of "me first."

Cooperation is the art of compromising on little things while keeping your eye on the big thing: your relationship.

Cooperative relationships grow and flourish over time. But, when couples fail to cooperate, they unintentionally sow seeds of dissatisfaction and disharmony.

If you're like most of us, you're probably a little bit headstrong: you probably want most things done in a fashion resembling the popular song "My Way." But, if you are observant, you will notice that those people who always insist upon "my way or the highway" usually end up with "the highway."

A better strategy for all concerned is to abandon the search for "my way" and search instead for "our way." That tune has a far happier ending. So today, tell your wife that you're serious about being a cooperative, solution-oriented husband, a man who's fully prepared to do his fair share, and then some. She needs to hear those words from you. Now.

Selfishness and marriage don't mix.

Marie T. Freeman

Husbands and wives who live happily ever after learn to give and take and to reach agreement by mutual consent. A man or woman with an unmovable backbone is in real trouble. God made backbones that can stand rigid but can also bend when necessary.

Vance Havner

Blessed are the peacemakers . . . .

Matthew 5:9 Holman CSB

Today's Prayer

Lord, so much more can be accomplished when we join together to fulfill our common goals and desires. As we seek to fulfill Your will for our lives, let us also join with others to accomplish Your greater good for our families, for our communities, for our nation, and for our world. Amen

Thanksgiving Yes . . . Envy No!

Stop your anger! Turn from your rage!
Do not envy others—it only leads to harm.
Psalm 37:8 NLT

As the recipient of God's grace, you have every reason to celebrate life. After all, God has promised you the opportunity to receive His abundance and His joy—in fact, you have the opportunity to receive those gifts right now. But if you or your wife allow envy to gnaw away at the fabric of your souls, you'll find that joy remains elusive. So do yourselves an enormous favor: Rather than succumbing to the sin of envy, focus on the marvelous things that God has done for you—starting with Christ's sacrifice. Thank the Giver of all good gifts, and keep thanking Him for the wonders of His love and the miracles of His creation. Count your own blessings and let your neighbors count theirs. It's the godly way to live.

Too many Christians envy the sinners their pleasures and the saint their joy, because they don't have either one.

Martin Luther

When you get hot under the collar, make sure your heart is prayer-conditioned.

Quips, Anonymous

When you worry about what you don't have, you won't be able to enjoy what you do have.

Charles Swindoll

A tranquil heart is life to the body, but jealousy is rottenness to the bones.

Proverbs 14:30 Holman CSB

Today's Prayer

Dear Lord, deliver me from the needless pain of envy. You have given me countless blessings. Let me be thankful for the gifts I have received, and let me never be resentful of the gifts You have given others. Amen

Walking in His Footsteps

I've laid down a pattern for you. What I've done, you do.
John 13:15 MSG

Jesus walks with you and your wife. Are you walking with Him? Hopefully, you will choose to walk with Him today and every day of your life.

Jesus loved you so much that He endured unspeakable humiliation and suffering for you. How will you respond to Christ's sacrifice? Will you take up His cross and follow Him (Luke 9:23), or will you choose another path? When you place your hopes squarely at the foot of the cross, when you place Jesus squarely at the center of your life, you will be blessed.

The old familiar hymn begins, "What a friend we have in Jesus . . . ." No truer words were ever penned. Jesus is the sovereign Friend and ultimate Savior of mankind. Christ showed enduring love for His believers by willingly sacrificing His own life so that we might have eternal life. Now, it is our turn to become His friend.

Let us love our Savior, let us praise Him, and let us share His message of salvation with the world. When we do, we demonstrate that our acquaintance with the Master is not a passing fancy, but is, instead, the cornerstone and the touchstone of our lives.

To walk out of His will is to walk into nowhere.

C. S. Lewis

Imagine the spiritual strength the disciples drew from walking hundreds of miles with Jesus . . . 3 John 4.

Jim Maxwell

A believer comes to Christ; a disciple follows after Him.

Vance Havner

If anyone would come after me, he must deny himself and take up his cross and follow me.

Mark 8:34 NIV

Today's Prayer

Dear Lord, we have heard Your Word, and we have felt Your presence in our hearts; let us act accordingly. Let our words and deeds serve as a testimony to the changes You have made in our lives. Let us praise You, Father, by following in the footsteps of Your Son, and let others see Him through us. Amen

In His Hands

For I know the thoughts that I think toward you, says the Lord, thoughts of peace and not of evil, to give you a future and a hope. Then you will call upon Me and go and pray to Me, and I will listen to you.

Jeremiah 29:11-12 NKJV

Sometimes the future seems bright, and sometimes it does not. Yet even when we cannot see the possibilities of tomorrow, God can. Our challenge is to trust ourselves to do the best work we can, and then to trust God to do the rest.

When we trust God, we should trust Him without reservation. We should steel ourselves against the inevitable disappointments of the day, secure in the knowledge that our Heavenly Father has a plan for the future that is brighter than we can imagine.

Are you and your wife willing to look to the future with trust and confidence? Hopefully so, because the future should not to be feared, it should be embraced. And it most certainly should be embraced by both of you.

That we may not complain of what is, let us see God's hand in all events; and, that we may not be afraid of what shall be, let us see all events in God's hand.

Matthew Henry

Hoping for a good future without investing in today is like a farmer waiting for a crop without ever planting any seed.

John Maxwell

Tomorrow's history has already been written—at the name of Jesus every knee must bow.

Paul E. Kauffman

Don't brashly announce what you're going to do tomorrow; you don't know the first thing about tomorrow.

Proverbs 27:1 MSG

Today's Prayer

Lord, sometimes life is so difficult that the future seems foreboding. And sometimes my wife and I may lose hope. But with You, there is always hope. Today, let us keep Your promises in our hearts, and let us trust the future to You. Amen

His Rule, Your Rule

*So in everything, do to others what you would have them
do to you, for this sums up the Law and the Prophets.*

Matthew 7:12 NIV

I s the Golden Rule one of the rules that governs your
household? Hopefully so. Obeying the Golden Rule is
a proven way to improve any relationship, including
your marriage. But the reverse is also true: if you or your
spouse ignore the Golden Rule altogether, you're headed
for trouble, and fast.

Too many marriages become unbalanced when one
partner assumes the role of the "taker" while the other
partner accepts the role of the "giver." But the healthiest
marriages are those in which both parties seek to give
more than they get.

Jesus made Himself perfectly clear: He instructed us to
treat others in the same way that we want to be treated.
That means that we must treat other people (including
our loved ones) with respect, kindness, and courtesy.

So if you're wondering how you should treat your
wife (or anyone else, for that matter), ask the person you
see every time you look into the mirror. The answer you
receive will tell you exactly what to do.

It is wrong for anyone to be anxious to receive more from his neighbor than he himself is willing to give to God.

St. Francis of Assisi

We should behave to our friends as we would wish our friends to behave to us.

Aristotle

To keep the Golden Rule we must put ourselves in other people's places, but to do that consists in and depends upon picturing ourselves in their places.

Harry Emerson Fosdick

Let us not become weary in doing good, for at the proper time we will reap a harvest if we do not give up.

Galatians 6:9 NIV

Today's Prayer

Dear Lord, we thank You for friends and family members who practice the Golden Rule. Because we expect to be treated with kindness, let us be kind. Because we wish to be loved, let us be loving. Because we need forgiveness, let us be merciful. In matters great and small, let us live by the Golden Rule, and let us express our gratitude to those who offer kindness and generosity to us. Amen

Taking Up the Cross

Then He said to them all, "If anyone wants to come with Me, he must deny himself, take up his cross daily, and follow Me."

Luke 9:23 Holman CSB

When Jesus addressed His disciples, He warned them that each one must, "take up his cross daily and follow me" (Luke 9:23 NIV). Christ's message was clear: in order to follow Him, Christ's disciples must deny themselves and, instead, trust Him completely. Nothing has changed since then.

When we have been saved by Christ, we can, if we choose, become passive Christians. We can sit back, secure in our own salvation, and let other believers spread the healing message of Jesus. But to do so is wrong. Instead, we are commanded to become disciples of the One who has saved us.

Do you seek to fulfill God's purpose for your life? Then follow Christ. Follow Him by picking up His cross today and every day that you live. Then, you will quickly discover that Christ's love has the power to change everything, including your marriage and your life.

There is not Christianity without a cross, for you cannot be a disciple of Jesus without taking up your cross.

Henry Blackaby

If we would be followers of Christ, indeed we must become personally and vitally involved in His death and resurrection. And this requires repentance, prayer, watchfulness, self-denial, detachment from the world, humility, obedience, and cross carrying.

A. W. Tozer

On the road to the Cross, it's only the first few yards that hurt.

St. John Vianney

You did not choose Me, but I chose you. I appointed you that you should go out and produce fruit, and that your fruit should remain, so that whatever you ask the Father in My name, He will give you.

John 15:16 Holman CSB

Today's Prayer

Help me, Lord, to understand what cross I am to carry today. And give me the strength and the courage to carry that cross along the path of Your choosing so that I may be a worthy husband and a worthy disciple of Your Son. Amen

He Is Here

Where can I go from your Spirit? Where can I flee from
your presence? If I go up to the heavens, you are there;
if I make my bed in the depths, you are there.
If I rise on the wings of the dawn, if I settle on the far side
of the sea, even there your hand will guide me,
your right hand will hold me fast.
Psalm 139:7-10 NIV

I f God is everywhere, why does He sometimes seem so far away? The answer to that question, of course, has nothing to do with God and everything to do with us.

When we begin each day on our knees, in praise and worship to Him, God often seems very near indeed. But, if we ignore God's presence or—worse yet—rebel against it altogether, the world in which we live becomes a spiritual wasteland.

Today, and every day hereafter, thank God and praise Him. He is the Giver of all things good. Wherever you are, whether you are happy or sad, victorious or vanquished, celebrate God's presence. And be comforted. For He is here.

It's been said that when God sends you on a journey, He will direct your path and light your way, even if it's only one step at a time. And from walking the mountains and valleys of my own life, I believe that to be true. When the Lord is with me, I can feel His presence and move out in confidence, and although I may not know my final destination, I have His assurance that I'm heading in the right direction.

Al Green

If only we would stop lamenting and look up, God is here. Christ is risen. The Spirit has been poured out from on high.

A. W. Tozer

Come near to God, and God will come near to you. You sinners, clean sin out of your lives. You who are trying to follow God and the world at the same time, make your thinking pure.

James 4:8 NCV

Today's Prayer

Heavenly Father, even when it seems to us that You are far away, You never leave our sides. Today and every day, let us strive to feel Your presence, and let us strive to sense Your love for our family and Your love for our world. Amen

Day 64

The Self-fulfilling Prophecy

Let us hold on to the confession of our hope without wavering, for He who promised is faithful.

Hebrews 10:23 Holman CSB

The self-fulfilling prophecy is alive, well, and living at your house. If you trust God and have faith for the future, your optimistic beliefs will give you direction and motivation. That's one reason that you should never lose hope, but certainly not the only reason. The primary reason that you, as a believer, should never lose hope, is because of God's unfailing promises.

Make no mistake about it: thoughts are powerful things: your thoughts have the power to lift you up or to hold you down. When you acquire the habit of hopeful thinking, you will have acquired a powerful tool for improving your life. So if you fall into the habit of negative thinking, think again. After all, God's Word teaches us that Christ can overcome every difficulty (John 16:33). And when God makes a promise, He keeps it.

Our hope in Christ for the future is the mainstream of our joy.

C. H. Spurgeon

What oxygen is to the lungs, such is hope to the meaning of life.

Emil Brunner

I wish I could make it all new again; I can't. But God can. "He restores my soul," wrote the shepherd. God doesn't reform; he restores. He doesn't camouflage the old; he restores the new. The Master Builder will pull out the original plan and restore it. He will restore the vigor; he will restore the energy. He will restore the hope. He will restore the soul.

Max Lucado

Be of good courage, and he shall strengthen your heart, all ye that hope in the LORD.

Psalm 31:24 KJV

Today's Prayer

Dear Lord, make me a hope-filled Christian. If I become discouraged, let me turn to You. If I grow weary, let me seek strength in You. In every aspect of my life, I will trust You, Father, today and forever. Amen

Day 65

A Dose of Laughter

A happy heart is like good medicine.
Proverbs 17:22 NCV

The old saying is true: "He who laughs, lasts." And the same can be said for couples. Laughter is not only tonic for our souls, it is also medicine for our marriages. But sometimes, amid the stresses of the day, we forget to take our medicine. Instead of viewing our lives with a mixture of optimism and humor, we begin to take things a little too seriously by allowing worries and distractions to rob us of the joy that God intends for our lives.

So the next time you and your wife begin to dwell upon the negatives of life, refocus your attention to things positive. The next time you find yourself falling prey to the blight of pessimism, stop yourself and turn your thoughts around. And, if you see your glass as "half-empty," rest assured that your spiritual vision is impaired. With God, your glass is never half-empty. With God as your protector and Christ as your Savior, your glass is filled to the brim and overflowing . . . forever.

Today, as a gift to yourself and to your beloved, approach life with a smile on your lips and hope in your heart. And laugh every chance you get. After all, God created laughter for a reason . . . and Father indeed knows best. So laugh often and, more importantly, laugh together!

Mirth is God's medicine. Everybody ought to bathe in it.

Henry Ward Beecher

I think everybody ought to be a laughing Christian. I'm convinced that there's just one place where there's not any laughter, and that's hell.

Jerry Clower

It is often just as sacred to laugh as it is to pray.

Charles Swindoll

A happy heart makes the face cheerful . . . .

Proverbs 15:13 NIV

Today's Prayer

Lord, when we begin to take ourselves or our lives too seriously, let us laugh. When we rush from place to place, slow us down, Lord, and let us laugh. Put a smile on our faces, Dear Lord, and let my wife and I share that smile with all who cross our paths. Amen

Solving Problems

People who do what is right may have many problems,
but the Lord will solve them all.

Psalm 34:19 NCV

From time to time, all of us face problems, disappointments, heartaches, and loss. Old Man Trouble pays periodic visits to each of us; none of us are exempt, and neither are our marriages. When we are troubled, God stands ready and willing to protect us. Our responsibility, of course, is to ask for His healing touch. When we call upon Him in heartfelt prayer, He will answer—in His own time and in accordance with His own perfect plan.

When we encounter problems or misunderstandings in our relationships, we must work to heal those problems sooner rather than later. Marital problems, like all problems, are most easily solved when they are new and small. That's why wise couples do the hard work of addressing their problems honestly, forthrightly, and quickly (even when they might prefer to downplay their difficulties or ignore those difficulties altogether).

Ignoring problems instead of fixing them is tempting

but irresponsible. After all, if we won't solve our problems, who will? Or should?

In summary, the hallmark of a healthy marriage is not the absence of problems, but a willingness to solve those problems now. May you live—and love—accordingly.

We are all faced with a series of great opportunities, brilliantly disguised as unsolvable problems. Unsolvable without God's wisdom, that is.

Charles Swindoll

You've got problems; I've got problems; all God's children have got problems. The question is how are you going to deal with them?

John Maxwell

But whoever listens to me will live securely and be free from the fear of danger.

Proverbs 1:33 Holman CSB

Today's Prayer

Lord, sometimes our problems are simply too big for us, but they are never too big for You. We will turn our troubles over to You, Lord, and we will trust You today and for all eternity. Amen

Discovering God's Plans

It is God who is at work in you,
both to will and to work for His good pleasure.

Philippians 2:13 NASB

God has plans for your life and your marriage, but He won't force those plans upon you. To the contrary, He has given you free will, the ability to make decisions on your own. With that freedom to choose comes the responsibility of living with the consequences of the choices you make.

If you seek to live in accordance with God's will for your life—and you should—then you will live in accordance with His commandments. You will study God's Word, and you will be watchful for His signs. You will associate with fellow Christians who will encourage your spiritual growth, and you will listen to that inner voice that speaks to you in the quiet moments of your daily devotionals.

God intends to use you in wonderful, unexpected ways if you let Him. The decision to seek God's plan and to follow it is yours and yours alone. The consequences of that decision have implications that are both profound and eternal, so choose carefully.

Every man's life is a plan of God.

Horace Bushnell

If not a sparrow falls upon the ground without your Father, you have reason to see that the smallest events of your career and your life are arranged by him.

C. H. Spurgeon

God is preparing you as his chosen arrow. As yet your shaft is hidden in his quiver, in the shadows, but, at the precise moment, he will reach for you and launch you to that place of his appointment.

Charles Swindoll

Trust the Lord your God with all your heart and lean not on your own understanding; in all your ways acknowledge him, and he will make your paths straight.

Proverbs 3:5-6 NIV

Today's Prayer

Dear Lord, You created us for a reason. And You brought my wife and me together for a reason. Give us the wisdom to follow Your direction for our journey. Let us do Your work here on earth by seeking Your will and living it, knowing that when we trust in You, Father, we are eternally blessed. Amen

The Simple Life

*Whoever becomes simple and elemental again, like this child,
will rank high in God's kingdom.*

Matthew 18:4 MSG

You and your wife live in a world where simplicity is in short supply. Think for a moment about the complexity of your everyday lives and compare it to the lives of your ancestors. Certainly, you are the beneficiary of many technological innovations, but those innovations have a price: in all likelihood, your world is highly complex.

Unless you take firm control of your time and your life, you may be overwhelmed by an ever-increasing tidal wave of complexity that threatens your happiness. But your Heavenly Father understands the joy of living simply, and so should you. So do yourself a favor: keep your life as simple as possible. Simplicity is, indeed, genius. By simplifying your life, you are destined to improve it.

Prescription for a happier and healthier life: resolve to slow down your pace; learn to say no gracefully; resist the temptation to chase after more pleasure, more hobbies, and more social entanglements.

James Dobson

It is part of Satan's program to make our faith complicated and involved. Now and then, we need a rediscovery of the simplicity that is in Christ and in our faith in Him.

Vance Havner

Simplicity reaches out after God; purity discovers and enjoys him.

Thomas à Kempis

He sent them off with these instructions: "Don't think you need a lot of extra equipment for this. You are the equipment. No special appeals for funds. Keep it simple."

Mark 6:8 MSG

Today's Prayer

Lord, help us see the wisdom of keeping things simple. When we complicate our lives, give me the wisdom to simplify. The world values complexity, Father, but You do not. Today, let my wife and me keep our thoughts focused intently on Your Word, on Your love, and on Your Son. Amen

Beyond Guilt

*There is therefore now no condemnation to those who are in
Christ Jesus, who do not walk according to the flesh,
but according to the Spirit.*

Romans 8:1 NKJV

All of us have sinned. Sometimes our sins result from our own stubborn rebellion against God's commandments. And sometimes, we are swept up in events that are beyond our abilities to control. Under either set of circumstances, we may experience intense feelings of guilt. But God has an answer for the guilt that we feel. That answer, of course, is His forgiveness. When we confess our wrongdoings and repent from them, we are forgiven by the One who created us.

Are you troubled by feelings of guilt or regret? If so, you must repent from your misdeeds, and you must ask your Heavenly Father for His forgiveness. When you do so, He will forgive you completely and without reservation. Then, you must forgive yourself just as God has forgiven you: thoroughly and unconditionally.

You never lose the love of God. Guilt is the warning that temporarily you are out of touch.

Jack Dominian

Spiritual life without guilt would be like physical life without pain. Guilt is a defense mechanism; it's like an alarm that goes off to lead you to confession when you sin.

John MacArthur

Let's take Jesus at this word. When he says we're forgiven, let's unload the guilt. When he says we're valuable, let's believe him. When he says we're eternal, let's bury our fear. When he says we're provided for, let's stop worrying.

Max Lucado

Work hard for sin your whole life and your pension is death. But God's gift is real life, eternal life, delivered by Jesus, our Master.

Romans 6:23 MSG

Today's Prayer

Dear Lord, thank You for the guilt that we feel when we disobey You. Help us confess our wrongdoings, help us accept Your forgiveness, and help us renew our passion to serve You. Amen

Day 70

He Offers Peace

Peace I leave with you; My peace I give to you;
not as the world gives do I give to you.
Do not let your heart be troubled, nor let it be fearful.
John 14:27 NASB

We are imperfect human beings who possess imperfect faith. So it's not surprising that we lose hope from time to time. When we do, we need the encouragement of friends and the life-changing power of prayer.

The beautiful words of John 14:27 remind us that Jesus offers us peace, not as the world gives, but as He alone gives.

Have you found the genuine peace that can be yours through Jesus Christ? Or are you still rushing after the illusion of "peace and happiness" that the world promises but cannot deliver?

Today, as a gift to yourself, to your wife, to your family, and to your friends, claim the inner peace that is your spiritual birthright: the peace of Jesus Christ. It is offered freely; it has been paid for in full; it is yours for the asking. So ask. And then share.

Christ alone can bring lasting peace—peace with God—peace among men and nations—and peace within our hearts.

Billy Graham

God cannot give us happiness and peace apart from Himself, because it is not there. There is no such thing.

C. S. Lewis

"My peace I give unto you"; it is a peace all over from the crown of the head to the sole of the feet, an irrepressible confidence.

Oswald Chambers

These things I have spoken to you, that in Me you may have peace. In the world you will have tribulation; but be of good cheer, I have overcome the world.

John 16:33 NKJV

Today's Prayer

Dear Lord, let us accept the peace and abundance that You offer through Your Son Jesus. You are the Giver of all things good, Father, and You give us peace when we draw close to You. Help us to trust Your will, to follow Your commands, and to accept Your peace, today and forever. Amen

Observing the Sabbath

Remember the Sabbath day, to keep it holy.
Exodus 20:8 NKJV

When God gave Moses the Ten Commandments, it became perfectly clear that our Heavenly Father intends for us to make the Sabbath a holy day, a day for worship, for contemplation, for fellowship, and for rest. Yet we live in a seven-day-a-week world, a world that all too often treats Sunday as a regular workday.

How does your family observe the Lord's day? When church is over, do you treat Sunday like any other day of the week? If so, it's time to think long and hard about your family's schedule and your family's priorities.

Whenever we ignore God's commandments, we pay a price. So if you've been treating Sunday as just another day, it's time to break that habit. When Sunday rolls around, don't try to fill every spare moment. Take time to rest . . . Father's orders!

Worship is not taught from the pulpit. It must be learned in the heart.

Jim Elliot

Worship is a daunting task. Each worships differently. But each should worship.

Max Lucado

There is no division into sacred and secular; it is all one great, glorious life.

Oswald Chambers

God has promised to give you all of eternity. The least you can do is give Him one day a week in return.

Marie T. Freeman

You may work for six days each week, but on the seventh day all work must come to a complete stop. It is the LORD's Sabbath day of complete rest, a holy day to assemble for worship. It must be observed wherever you live.

Leviticus 23:3 NLT

Today's Prayer

Dear Lord, I thank You for the Sabbath day, a day when my family and I can worship You and praise Your Son. We will keep the Sabbath as a holy day, a day when we can honor You. Amen

Beyond Bitterness

All bitterness, anger and wrath, insult and slander must be
removed from you, along with all wickedness.
And be kind and compassionate to one another, forgiving one
another, just as God also forgave you in Christ.

Ephesians 4:31-32 Holman CSB

The world holds few if any rewards for husbands and wives who remain angrily focused upon the past. Still, the act of forgiveness is difficult for all but the most saintly men and women. Are you mired in the quicksand of bitterness or regret? If so, you are not only disobeying God's Word, you are also wasting your time.

Being frail, fallible, imperfect human beings, most of us are quick to anger, quick to blame, slow to forgive, and even slower to forget. Yet as Christians, we are commanded to forgive others, just as we, too, have been forgiven.

If there exists even one person—including your spouse—against whom you hold bitter feelings, it's time to forgive. Or, if you are embittered against yourself for some past mistake or shortcoming, it's finally time to forgive yourself and move on. Hatred, bitterness, and regret are not part of God's plan for your life. Forgiveness is.

Bitterness is a spiritual sickness. It will consume your soul; it is dangerous to your emotional health; it can undermine your marriage if you let it . . . so don't let it!

Be so preoccupied with good will that you haven't room for ill will.

E. Stanley Jones

Acrid bitterness inevitably seeps into the lives of people who harbor grudges and suppress anger, and bitterness is always a poison.

Lee Strobel

Don't insist on getting even; that's not for you to do. "I'll do the judging," says God. "I'll take care of it."

Romans 12:19 MSG

Today's Prayer

Heavenly Father, free our marriage from all bitterness and resentment. When we are angry, we cannot feel Your peace. When we are bitter, we cannot sense Your presence. Let us turn away from bitterness and regret as we claim the spiritual abundance that You offer through the gift of Your Son. Amen

151

The Fear Factor

But Jesus immediately said to them:
"Take courage! It is I. Don't be afraid."
Matthew 14:27 NIV

Christian couples have every reason to live courageously. After all, the ultimate battle has already been fought and won on the cross at Calvary. But, even dedicated followers of Christ may find their courage tested by the inevitable disappointments and tragedies that occur in the lives of believers and non-believers alike.

Every human life is a tapestry of events: some wonderful, some not-so-wonderful, and some downright disheartening. When the storm clouds form overhead and we find ourselves wandering through the dark valley of despair, our faith is stretched, sometimes to the breaking point. But as believers, we can be comforted: Wherever we find ourselves, whether at the top of the mountain or the depths of the valley, God is there, and because He cares for us, we can live courageously.

The next time you find yourself in a fear-provoking situation, remember that God is as near as your next breath, and remember that He offers salvation to His children. He is your shield and your strength; He is your protector and your deliverer. Call upon Him in your hour of need and then be comforted. Whatever your challenge, whatever your trouble, God can handle it. And will.

Down through the centuries, in times of trouble and trial, God has brought courage to the hearts of those who love Him. The Bible is filled with assurances of God's help and comfort in every kind of trouble.

Billy Graham

To fear and not be afraid, that is the paradox of faith.

A. W. Tozer

The LORD himself goes before you and will be with you; he will never leave you nor forsake you. Do not be afraid; do not be discouraged.

Deuteronomy 31:8 NIV

Today's Prayer

Lord, sometimes, this world is a fearful place. Yet, You have promised that You are always with us. Because You are our protector, we are not afraid. Today, Dear Lord, my wife and I will live courageously as we place our trust in Your everlasting promises and in Your everlasting love. Amen

A Series of Choices

The thing you should want most is God's kingdom
and doing what God wants.
Then all these other things you need will be given to you.
Matthew 6:33 NCV

Your life is a series of choices. From the instant you wake up in the morning until the moment you nod off to sleep at night, you make countless decisions—decisions about the things you do, decisions about the words you speak, and decisions about the way that you choose to direct your thoughts.

As a believer who has been transformed by the love of Jesus, you have every reason to make wise choices. But sometimes, when the daily grind threatens to grind you up and spit you out, you may make choices that are displeasing to God. When you do, you'll pay a price because you'll forfeit the happiness and the peace that might otherwise have been yours.

So, as you pause to consider the kind of Christian you are—and the kind of Christian you want to become—ask yourself whether you're sitting on the fence or standing in the light. The choice is yours . . . and so are the consequences.

The greatest choice any man makes is to let God choose for him.

Vance Havner

Life is pretty much like a cafeteria line—it offers us many choices, both good and bad. The Christian must have a spiritual radar that detects the difference not only between bad and good but also among good, better, and best.

Dennis Swanberg

Every day, I find countless opportunities to decide whether I will obey God and demonstrate my love for Him or try to please myself or the world system. God is waiting for my choices.

Bill Bright

I am offering you life or death, blessings or curses. Now, choose life! . . . To choose life is to love the Lord your God, obey him, and stay close to him.

Deuteronomy 30:19-20 NCV

Today's Prayer

Heavenly Father, I have many choices to make. Help me choose wisely as I care for my wife and family. And let me follow in the footsteps of Your only begotten Son today and every day. Amen

Day 75

Confidence Restored

I've told you all this so that trusting me, you will be
unshakable and assured, deeply at peace. In this godless world
you will continue to experience difficulties.
But take heart! I've conquered the world.

John 16:33 MSG

Are you a confident, faithful believer, or do you live under a cloud of uncertainty and doubt? As a Christian, you have many reasons to be confident. After all, God is in His heaven; Christ has risen; and you are the recipient of God's grace. Despite these blessings, you may, from time to time, find yourself being tormented by negative emotions—and you are certainly not alone.

Even the most faithful Christians are overcome by occasional bouts of fear and doubt. You and your wife are no different. But even when you feel very distant from God, remember that God is never distant from you. When you sincerely seek His presence, He will touch your heart, calm your fears, and restore your confidence.

Pessimism is intellectual poison. And negativity has the power to harm your heart if you let it. So if you've allowed negative thoughts to creep into your minds and hearts, here's your assignment: Start spending more time thinking about your blessings and less time fretting about your hardships . . . starting now.

God's omniscience can instill you with a supernatural confidence that can transform your life.

Bill Hybels

Believe and do what God says. The life-changing consequences will be limitless, and the results will be confidence and peace of mind.

Franklin Graham

Bible hope is confidence in the future.

Warren Wiersbe

You are my hope; O Lord GOD, You are my confidence.

Psalm 71:5 NASB

Today's Prayer

Lord, You are my Savior and my Sustainer. I will be safe with You in heaven, and I am safe with You here on earth. Today, I will trust in Your promises. And because of my trust in You, Father, I can be a confident husband and a purposeful servant to Your Son. Amen

The Temptation to Judge

How can you say to your brother, "Brother, let me take out
the speck that is in your eye," when you yourself don't see
the log in your eye? Hypocrite! First take the log
out of your eye, and then you will see clearly to take out
the speck in your brother's eye.

Luke 6:42 Holman CSB

Even the most dedicated Christian couples may fall prey to a powerful yet subtle temptation: the temptation to judge others. But as Christians, we are commanded to refrain from such behavior. The warning of Matthew 7:1 is clear: "Judge not, that ye be not judged" (KJV). Yet, as fallible, imperfect human beings living in a stressful world, we are sorely tempted to do otherwise.

As Jesus came upon a young woman who had been condemned by the Pharisees, He spoke not only to the crowd that was gathered there, but also to all generations when He warned, "He that is without sin among you, let him first cast a stone at her" (John 8:7 KJV). Christ's message is clear, and it applies not only to the Pharisees of ancient times, but also to us.

We have all fallen short of God's commandments, and none of us, therefore, are qualified to "cast the first stone."

Thankfully, God has forgiven us, and we, too, must forgive others. As Christian believers, we are warned that to judge others is to invite fearful consequences: to the extent we judge others, so, too, will we be judged by God. Let us refrain, then, from judging our neighbors. Instead, let us forgive them and love them in the same way that God has forgiven us.

Being critical of others, including God, is one way we try to avoid facing and judging our own sins.

Warren Wiersbe

Do not judge, or you too will be judged. For in the same way you judge others, you will be judged, and with the measure you use, it will be measured to you.

Matthew 7:1 NIV

Today's Prayer

Dear Lord, sometimes we are quick to judge others. But, You have commanded us not to judge. Keep us mindful, Father, that when we judge others, we are living outside Your will for our lives. You have forgiven us, Lord. Let us forgive others, let us love them, and let us help them . . . without judging them. Amen

God's Guidebook

*You will be a good servant of Christ Jesus, constantly
nourished on the words of the faith and of the sound doctrine
which you have been following.*

1 Timothy 4:6 NASB

D o you read your Bible a lot . . . or not? The
answer to this simple question will determine, to
a surprising extent, the quality of your life, the
direction of your faith, and the condition of your marriage.

As you establish priorities for life, you must decide
whether God's Word will be a bright spotlight that guides
your path every day or a tiny nightlight that occasionally
flickers in the dark. The decision to study the Bible—or
not—is yours and yours alone. But make no mistake: how
you choose to use your Bible will have a profound impact
on you and your loved ones.

The Bible is the ultimate guide for life; make it your
guidebook as well. When you do, you can be comforted in
the knowledge that your steps are guided by a Source of
wisdom and truth that never fails.

Reading news without reading the Bible will inevitably lead to an unbalanced life, an anxious spirit, a worried and depressed soul.

Bill Bright

The Bible is a Christian's guidebook, and I believe the knowledge it sheds on pain and suffering is the great antidote to fear for suffering people. Knowledge can dissolve fear as light destroys darkness.

Philip Yancey

The Bible is the treasure map that leads us to God's highest treasure: eternal life.

Max Lucado

For I am not ashamed of the gospel of Christ, for it is the power of God to salvation for everyone who believes.

Romans 1:16 NKJV

Today's Prayer

As my wife and I journey through this life, Lord, help us always to consult the true road map: Your Holy Word. We know that when we turn our hearts and our thoughts to You, Father, You will lead us along the path that is right for us. Today, Dear Lord, let us know Your will and study Your Word so that we might understand Your plan for our lives. Amen

A Man of Prayer

Rejoice always, pray without ceasing,
in everything give thanks;
for this is the will of God in Christ Jesus for you.
1 Thessalonians 5:16-18 NKJV

I s prayer an integral part of your daily life, or is it a
hit-or-miss habit? Do you "pray without ceasing," or
is your prayer life an afterthought? Do you regularly
pray in the solitude of the early morning darkness, or do
you lower your head only when others are watching? The
answer to these questions will determine the direction of
your day—and your life.

So here's your challenge: during the next year, make
yourself a man of prayer. Begin your prayers early in the
morning and continue them throughout the day. And
remember this: God does answer your prayers, but He's not
likely to answer those prayers until you've prayed them.

Prayer is getting into perfect communion with God.

Oswald Chambers

Men may reject our appeals, reject our message, oppose our arguments, despise our persons—but they are helpless against our prayers.

J. Sidlow Baxter

You don't need fancy words or religious phrases. Just tell God the way it really is.

Jim Cymbala

Prayer will make a man cease from sin, or sin will entice a man to cease from prayer.

John Bunyan

Ask and it shall be given to you; seek and you shall find; knock and it shall be opened to you. For every one who asks receives, and he who seeks finds, and to him who knocks it shall be opened.

Matthew 7:7-8 NASB

Today's Prayer

Lord, make me a man of prayer. Give me the wisdom to consult You often; give me the insight to hear Your voice; and give me the courage to follow Your path, this day and every day. Amen

A Life of Fulfillment

For You, O God, have tested us; You have refined us as silver
is refined . . . we went through fire and through water;
but You brought us out to rich fulfillment.

Psalm 66:10–12 NKJV

Everywhere we turn, or so it seems, the world promises fulfillment, contentment, and happiness. But the contentment that the world offers is fleeting and incomplete. Thankfully, the fulfillment that God offers is all encompassing and everlasting.

Sometimes, amid the inevitable hustle and bustle of life-here-on-earth, you and your wife may forfeit—albeit temporarily—the joy of Christ as you wrestle with the challenges of daily living. Yet God's Word is clear: fulfillment through Christ is available to all who seek it and claim it. Count yourself among that number. Seek first a personal, transforming relationship with Jesus, and then claim the joy, the fulfillment, and the spiritual abundance that the Shepherd offers His sheep.

Find satisfaction in him who made you, and only then find satisfaction in yourself as part of his creation.

St. Augustine

We are never more fulfilled than when our longing for God is met by His presence in our lives.

Billy Graham

Our sense of joy, satisfaction, and fulfillment in life increases, no matter what the circumstances, if we are in the center of God's will.

Billy Graham

Abundant peace belongs to those who love Your instruction; nothing makes them stumble.

Psalm 119:165 Holman CSB

Today's Prayer

Dear Lord, when my wife and I turn our thoughts and prayers to You, we feel peace and fulfillment. But sometimes, when we are distracted by the busyness of the day, fulfillment seems far away. Today, let us trust Your will, let us follow Your commands, and let us accept Your peace. Amen

God Is Love

God is love; and he that dwelleth in love dwelleth in God,
and God in him.

1 John 4:16 KJV

God is love. It's a sweeping statement, a profoundly important description of what God is and how God works. God's love is perfect. When we open our hearts to His perfect love, we are touched by the Creator's hand, and we are transformed.

Today, even if you can only carve out a few quiet moments, offer sincere prayers of thanksgiving to your Father. Thank Him for His blessings and His love. As you sit in silence, open your heart to the Father, and do your best to sense His presence. When you do, you'll discover the genuine peace that only the Creator can provide. That peace, of course, flows from the loving heart of God. You can experience His peace and His love today . . . and you should.

The life of faith is a daily exploration of the constant and countless ways in which God's grace and love are experienced.

Eugene Peterson

The greatest love of all is God's love for us, a love that showed itself in action.

Billy Graham

If it is maintained that anything so small as the Earth must, in any event, be too unimportant to merit the love of the Creator, we reply that no Christian ever supposed we did merit it. Christ did not die for men because they were intrinsically worth dying for, but because He is intrinsically love, and therefore loves infinitely.

C. S. Lewis

Unfailing love surrounds those who trust the LORD.

Psalm 32:10 NLT

Today's Prayer

Dear Heavenly Father, You have blessed us with a love that is infinite and eternal. We will be Your loving servants, Father, today and throughout eternity. And, we will show our love for You by sharing Your message and Your love with a world that desperately needs the healing touch of the Master's hand. Amen

He Renews Our Strength

Then He who sat on the throne said,
"Behold, I make all things new."
Revelation 21:5 NKJV

When we genuinely lift our hearts and prayers to God, He renews our strength. Are you almost too weary to lift your head? Then bow it. Offer your concerns and your fears to your Father in heaven. He is always at your side, offering His love and His strength.

God intends that you experience joy and abundance in every aspect of your life, including your marriage, but He will not force His joy upon you. You and your loved ones must claim God's abundance for yourself. So, today and every day hereafter, celebrate this life that God has given you by focusing your thoughts and your energies upon things that are positive. Today, count your blessings instead of your hardships. And thank the Giver of all things good for gifts that are simply too numerous to count . . . starting, of course, with your marriage.

God is not running an antique shop! He is making all things new!

Vance Havner

God specializes in taking bruised, soiled, broken, guilty, and miserable vessels and making them whole, forgiven, and useful again.

Charles Swindoll

The same voice that brought Lazarus out of the tomb raised us to newness of life.

C. H. Spurgeon

Create in me a clean heart, O God, and renew a steadfast spirit within me.

Psalm 51:10 NKJV

Today's Prayer

Heavenly Father, sometimes we are troubled, and sometimes we grow weary. When we are weak, Lord, give us strength. When we are discouraged, renew us. When we are fearful, let us feel Your healing touch. Let us always trust in Your promises, Lord, and let us draw strength from those promises and from Your unending love. Amen

Doing It Now

We can't afford to waste a minute, must not squander these
precious daylight hours in frivolity and indulgence . . . .
Don't loiter and linger, waiting until the very last minute.
Dress yourselves in Christ, and be up and about!
Romans 13:13-14 MSG

The habit of procrastination takes a two-fold toll on its victims. First, important work goes unfinished; second (and more importantly), valuable energy is wasted in the process of putting off the things that remain undone. Procrastination results from an individual's short-sighted attempt to postpone temporary discomfort. What results is a senseless cycle of 1. delay, followed by 2. worry followed by 3. a panicky and often futile attempt to "catch up." Procrastination is, at its core, a struggle against oneself; the only antidote is action.

Once you and your wife acquire the habit of doing what needs to be done when it needs to be done, you will avoid untold trouble, worry, and stress. So learn to defeat procrastination by paying less attention to your fears and more attention to your responsibilities. God has created a world that punishes procrastinators and rewards men who "do it now." Life doesn't procrastinate—neither should you.

Don't duck the most difficult problems. That just insures that the hardest part will be left when you're most tired. Get the big one done, and it's all downhill from then on.

Norman Vincent Peale

Do noble things, do not dream them all day long.

Charles Kingsley

Not now becomes never.

Martin Luther

Are there those among you who are truly wise and under-standing? Then they should show it by living right and doing good things with a gentleness that comes from wisdom.

James 3:13 NCV

Today's Prayer

Dear Lord, today is a new day. Help me tackle the important tasks immediately, even if those tasks are unpleasant. Don't let me put off until tomorrow what I should do today. Amen

Seeking God and Finding Happiness

But happy are those . . .
whose hope is in the LORD their God.
Psalm 146:5 NLT

God wants you and your wife to experience a happy marriage. And, of course, your intentions are the same. But how, exactly, can you experience the full measure of joy that God intends for you and your bride to share? A great place to start is by allowing yourself to become genuinely enthusiastic about your marriage and your life.

Are you excited about your marriage? Do you feel good about yourself, your wife, your kids, your friends, and your situation? And do you see each day as a glorious opportunity to serve God and to do His will? Hopefully so. After all, you were created in God's image, and He has blessed you in more ways than you can count. Now, it's your job to thank Him with words of praise and a life that is praiseworthy.

Psalm 100 reminds us that, as believers, we have every reason to celebrate: "Shout for joy to the LORD, all the earth. Worship the LORD with gladness" (v. 1-2 NIV). Yet sometimes, amid the inevitable hustle and bustle of life here on earth, we can forfeit—albeit temporarily—the joy that God intends for our lives.

Few things in life are more sad, or, for that matter, more absurd, than the sight of a grumpy Christian couple bickering their way through life. After all, Christ offers all His believers the possibility of joy and abundance—but He does not force His joy upon us. We must claim that joy for ourselves, as must our loved ones. When we do, Jesus, in turn, fills our spirits with His power and His love. Then, we can share Christ's joy and His message with a world that needs both.

God has charged Himself with full responsibility for our eternal happiness and stands ready to take over the management of our lives the moment we turn in faith to Him.

A. W. Tozer

Today's Prayer

Dear Lord, make me a happy husband. You have given me so many blessings, Father. Let me be a cheerful Christian as I share Your joy with my wife, with my family, with my friends, and with the world. Amen

Face-to-face with Old Man Trouble

These things I have spoken to you, that in Me you may
have peace. In the world you will have tribulation;
but be of good cheer, I have overcome the world.
John 16:33 NKJV

Every marriage, like every life, is destined to encounter days of hardship and pain. Throughout the seasons of life, we must all endure life-altering personal losses that leave us breathless. When we do, God stands ready to protect us. Psalm 147 promises, "He heals the brokenhearted, and binds their wounds" (v. 3 NASB). God keeps His promises. When we are troubled, we can call upon Him, and—in His own time and according to His own plan—He will heal us.

The fact that we encounter adversity is not nearly so important as the way we choose to deal with it. When tough times arrive, we have a clear choice: we can begin the difficult work of tackling our troubles . . . or not. When we summon the courage to look Old Man Trouble squarely in the eye, he usually blinks. But, if we refuse to address our problems, even the smallest annoyances have a way of growing into king-sized catastrophes.

Psalm 145 promises, "The Lord is near to all who call on him, to all who call on him in truth. He fulfills the desires of those who fear him; he hears their cry and saves them" (vv. 18-20 NIV). And remember John 16:33, the words of Jesus offer us comfort.

Are you and your spouse enduring tough times? If so, hold tightly to each other and trust in the promises of God. When you do, you may rest assured that the two of you—plus God—can handle anything that comes your way.

We are pressured in every way but not crushed; we are perplexed but not in despair.

2 Corinthians 4:8 Holman CSB

Today's Prayer

Lord, sometimes life is so difficult that we don't see hope for the future. But with You, there is always hope. Today, give my wife and me the courage to trust You completely. You are our protector, Dear Lord; we will praise You and we will trust in the perfect wisdom of Your plan for our lives. Amen

Live Optimistically

My cup runs over. Surely goodness and mercy
shall follow me all the days of my life;
and I will dwell in the house of the Lord Forever.
Psalm 23:5-6 NKJV

A re you and your wife optimistic, enthusiastic Christians? You should be. After all, as believers, you have every reason to be optimistic about life here on earth and life eternal. As C. H. Spurgeon observed, "Our hope in Christ for the future is the mainstream of our joy." But sometimes, you may find yourselves pulled down by the inevitable demands and worries of life here on earth. If you find yourselves discouraged, exhausted, or both, then it's time to take your concerns to God. When you do, He will lift your spirits and renew your strength.

Today, make this promise to yourselves and keep it: vow to be hope-filled Christians. Think optimistically about your marriage, your family, and your future. Trust your hopes, not your fears. Take time to celebrate God's glorious creation. And then, when you've filled your hearts with hope and gladness, share your optimism with others. They'll be better for it, and so will you.

The popular idea of faith is of a certain obstinate optimism: the hope, tenaciously held in the face of trouble, that the universe is fundamentally friendly and things may get better.

J. I. Packer

The people whom I have seen succeed best in life have always been cheerful and hopeful people who went about their business with a smile on their faces.

Charles Kingsley

Go forward confidently, energetically attacking problems, expecting favorable outcomes.

Norman Vincent Peale

No Christian can be a pessimist, for Christianity is a system of radical optimism.

William Ralph Inge

Encourage each other. Live in harmony and peace. Then the God of love and peace will be with you.

2 Corinthians 13:11 NLT

Today's Prayer

Thank You, Lord, for Your infinite love. Make us optimistic Christians, Father, as we place our hopes and our trust in You. Amen

The Love of Money

For the love of money is a root of all sorts of evil, and some by longing for it have wandered away from the faith and pierced themselves with many griefs.

1 Timothy 6:10 NASB

Our society is in love with money and the things that money can buy. God is not. God cares about people, not possessions, and so must we. We must, to the best of our abilities, love our neighbors as ourselves, and we must, to the best of our abilities, resist the mighty temptation to place possessions ahead of people.

Money, in and of itself, is not evil; worshipping money is. So today, as you and your wife prioritize matters of importance, remember that God is almighty, but the dollar is not.

If we worship God, we are blessed. But if we worship the almighty dollar, we are inevitably punished because of our misplaced priorities—and our punishment inevitably comes sooner rather than later.

God is looking over the entire earth for men who have the proper attitude toward money and who will use it according to His direction and not according to their own interests.

Larry Burkett

If the glories of heaven were more real to us, if we lived less for material things and more for things eternal and spiritual, we would be less easily disturbed in this present life.

Billy Graham

Money is a mirror that, strange as it sounds, reflects our personal weaknesses and strengths with amazing clarity.

Dave Ramsey

If your wealth increases, don't make it the center of your life.

Psalm 62:10 NLT

Today's Prayer

Dear Lord, we will earn money, and we will use money, but we will not worship money. Give my wife and me the wisdom and the discipline to be responsible stewards of our financial resources, and let us use those resources for the glory of Your kingdom. Amen

Purposeful Living

Whatever you do, do all to the glory of God.
1 Corinthians 10:31 NKJV

Each morning, as the sun rises in the east, you both welcome a new day, a day that is filled to the brim with opportunities, with possibilities, and with God. As you and your wife contemplate God's blessings in your own lives, you should prayerfully seek His guidance for the day ahead.

Discovering God's unfolding purpose for your marriage is a daily journey, a journey guided by the teachings of God's Holy Word. As you reflect upon God's promises and upon the meaning that those promises hold for each of you, ask God to lead you throughout the coming day. Let your Heavenly Father direct your steps; concentrate on what God wants you to do now, and leave the distant future in hands that are far more capable than your own: His hands.

The Christian life is not simply following principles but being empowered to fulfill our purpose: knowing and exalting Christ.

Franklin Graham

It is important to set goals because if you do not have a plan, a goal, a direction, a purpose, and a focus, you are not going to accomplish anything for the glory of God.

Bill Bright

Continually restate to yourself what the purpose of your life is.

Oswald Chambers

In Him we were also made His inheritance, predestined according to the purpose of the One who works out everything in agreement with the decision of His will.

Ephesians 1:11 Holman CSB

Today's Prayer

Dear Lord, You are the Creator of the universe, and we know that Your plan for our lives is grander than we can imagine. Let Your purposes be our purposes, and let us trust in the assurance of Your promises. Amen

Richly Blessed

God loves a cheerful giver.
2 Corinthians 9:7 NIV

Hymn writer Fanny Crosby wrote, "To God be the glory; great thing He hath done! So loved He the world that He gave us his son." God's love for us is so complete that He sent Jesus to this earth so that we, His believers, might have eternal life: "But God demonstrates his own love for us in this: While we were still sinners, Christ died for us" (Romans 5:8 NIV).

We, as Christ's followers, are challenged to share His love. We do so, in part, by dealing generously and lovingly with others.

When we walk each day with Christ—and obey the commandments found in God's Holy Word—we are worthy ambassadors for Him. Just as Christ has been— and will always be—the ultimate friend to His flock, so should we be Christlike in our love and generosity to those in pain and to those in need. When we share the love of Christ, we share a priceless gift; may we share it today and every day that we live.

A happy spirit takes the grind out of giving. The grease of gusto frees the gears of generosity.

Charles Swindoll

If you want to be truly happy, you won't find it on an endless quest for more stuff. You'll find it in receiving God's generosity and in passing that generosity along.

Bill Hybels

If you desire to become a more generous person, don't wait for your income to change. Change your heart.

John Maxwell

Let us give according to our incomes, lest God make our incomes match our gifts.

Peter Marshall

Based on the gift they have received, everyone should use it to serve others, as good managers of the varied grace of God.

1 Peter 4:10 Holman CSB

Today's Prayer

Dear Lord, You have been so generous with my wife and me; let us be generous with others. Help us to focus on the needs of others. And, make us humble givers, Lord, so that all the glory and the praise might be Yours. Amen

Day 89

We Are All Role Models

You are the light that gives light to the world . . . .
In the same way, you should be a light for other people.
Live so that they will see the good things you do
and will praise your Father in heaven.
Matthew 5:14,16 NCV

Whether you and your wife realize it or not, your marriage serves as a powerful example to family and friends. So here's the big question: what kind of example is your marriage? Is yours a marriage that honors God? Is it a marriage that strengthens the bonds of family? Is it a marriage that others should seek to emulate? If so, you are fortunate, you are wise, and you are blessed.

We live in a cynical, temptation-filled world where negative role models abound and positive role models are often in short supply. That's why your positive role model is so important. When you and your wife serve as positive examples for other couples, you are helping those couples visualize positive changes that they can make in their own marriages.

Phillips Brooks advised, "Be such a person, and live such a life, that if every person were such as you, and every

184

life a life like yours, this earth would be God's Paradise."
And that's sound advice because our families and friends
are watching . . . and so is God.

A man ought to live so that everybody knows he is a
Christian, and most of all, his family ought to know.

D. L. Moody

Our walk counts far more than our talk, always!

George Mueller

Your life will not convince those around you of the
reality of Jesus if you cannot live in unity with your fellow
Christians.

Henry Blackaby

*Set an example of good works yourself, with integrity and
dignity in your teaching.*

Titus 2:7 Holman CSB

Today's Prayer

Dear Lord, help me be an honorable husband and a
positive role model to others. Let the things that I say and
the things that I do show everyone what it means to be a
follower of Your Son. Amen

Day 90

Heeding God's Call

One thing I do, forgetting those things which are behind and
reaching forward to those things which are ahead,
I press toward the goal for the prize of the upward call
of God in Christ Jesus.

Philippians 3:13-14 NKJV

I t is vitally important that you heed God's call. In John 15:16, Jesus says, "You did not choose me, but I chose you and appointed you to go and bear fruit—fruit that will last" (NIV). In other words, you and your wife have been called by Christ, and now, it is up to you to decide precisely how you will answer.

When you align yourselves with God's purposes, you avail yourselves of His power and His peace. But how can you know precisely what God's intentions are? The answer, of course, is that even the most well-intentioned believers face periods of uncertainty and doubt about the direction of their lives. So, too, will you. When you arrive at one of life's inevitable crossroads, that is precisely the moment when you should turn your thoughts and prayers toward God. When you do, He will make Himself known to you in a time and manner of His choosing.

Have you and your wife already found your special calling? If so, you're a very lucky couple. If not, keep searching and keep praying until you discover it. And remember this: God has important work for you to do—work that no one else on earth can accomplish but you.

The place where God calls you is the place where your deep gladness and the world's deep hunger meet.

Frederick Buechner

That's plain enough, isn't it? You're no longer wandering exiles. This kingdom of faith is now your home country. You're no longer strangers or outsiders. You belong here, with as much right to the name Christian as anyone. God is building a home. He's using us all—irrespective of how we got here—in what he is building.

Ephesians 2:19 MSG

Today's Prayer

Heavenly Father, You have called my wife and me to do Your kingdom work, and we acknowledge that calling. In these quiet moments before this busy day unfolds, we come to You. We will study Your Word and seek Your guidance. Give us the wisdom to know Your will for our lives and the courage to follow wherever You may lead us, today and forever. Amen

A Passion for Life

He did it with all his heart. So he prospered.
2 Chronicles 31:21 NKJV

Are you and your wife passionate about your lives, your loved ones, your work, your marriage, and your Savior? You should be. As thoughtful Christians, you have every reason to live passionately, but sometimes the struggles of everyday living may leave you feeling discouraged, exhausted, or both.

If you fear that your passion for life is slowly fading away, it's time to slow down, to rest, to recount your blessings, to worship, and to pray. When you feel worried or weary, you must pray fervently for God to renew your sense of wonderment and excitement.

When you allow Christ to reign over your heart—when you worship Him with words, thoughts, prayers, and deeds—your life can become a glorious adventure. When you live passionately—and share your passion with others—God will most certainly bless you and yours . . . today and forever.

When we realize and embrace the Lord's will for us, we will love to do it. We won't want to do anything else. It's a passion.

Franklin Graham

If your heart has grown cold, it is because you have moved away from the fire of His presence.

Beth Moore

I don't know about you, but I want to do more than survive life—I want to mount up like the eagle and glide over rocky crags, nest in the tallest of trees, dive for nourishment in the deepest of mountain lakes, and soar on the wings of the wind.

Barbara Johnson

Everything you love is what makes a life worth living.

John Eldredge

Do not lack diligence; be fervent in spirit; serve the Lord.

Romans 12:11 Holman CSB

Today's Prayer

Dear Lord, we thank You for Your countless blessings. We will demonstrate our gratitude by living obediently and passionately. We praise You, Father, for Your blessings, for Your love, and for Your Son. Amen

Beyond Worry

But seek first the kingdom of God and His righteousness, and
all these things shall be added to you. Therefore do not worry
about tomorrow, for tomorrow will worry about its own
things. Sufficient for the day is its own trouble.

Matthew 6:33-34 NKJV

Because we are imperfect human beings struggling with imperfect circumstances, we worry. Even though we, as Christians, have the assurance of salvation—even though we, as Christians, have the promise of God's love and protection—we find ourselves fretting over the inevitable frustrations of everyday life (not to mention married life). Jesus understood our concerns when He spoke the reassuring words found in the 6th chapter of Matthew.

Where is the best place to take your worries? Take them to God. Take your troubles to Him; take your fears to Him; take your doubts to Him; take your weaknesses to Him; take your sorrows to Him . . . and leave them all there. Seek protection from the One who offers you eternal salvation; build your spiritual house upon the Rock that cannot be moved.

Perhaps you are concerned about your family, your future, your health, or your finances. Or perhaps you are simply a "worrier" by nature. If so, make Matthew 6 a regular part of your daily Bible reading. This beautiful passage will remind you that God still sits in His heaven and you are His beloved child. Then, perhaps, you will worry a little less and trust God a little more, and that's as it should be because God is trustworthy . . . and you are protected.

I've read the last page of the Bible. It's all going to turn out all right.

Billy Graham

Let not your heart be troubled; you believe in God, believe also in Me.

John 14:1 NKJV

Today's Prayer

Dear Lord, You understand our worries and our fears—and You forgive us when we are weak. When our faith begins to waver, Father, help us to trust You more. Then, with Your Holy Word on our lips and with the love of Your Son in our hearts, let us live courageously, faithfully, prayerfully, and thankfully today and every day. Amen

Investing the Time

To everything there is a season,
a time for every purpose under heaven.
Ecclesiastes 3:1 NKJV

I f you sincerely want your marriage to flourish, then you should be prepared to invest the time and energy required to do so. Wise couples invest time—high quality time—nurturing their relationships. And it shows.

Time is a precious, nonrenewable gift from God. But sometimes, we treat our time here on earth as if it were not a gift at all: We may be tempted to waste time in countless ways, and when we do so, we pay a high price for our mistaken priorities.

How are you choosing to spend the time that God has given you? Are you carving out large blocks of time to spend with your wife? Or are you wasting precious days rushing after the countless distractions and temptations that the world has to offer?

As you establish priorities for your day and your life, remember that each new day is a special treasure to be savored and celebrated with your loved ones. As a Christian couple, you and your wife have much to celebrate and much to do. It's up to both of you to honor God for the gift of time by using that gift wisely . . . and using it together.

The essence of the Christian life is Jesus: that in all things He might have the preeminence, not that in some things He might have a place.

Franklin Graham

Don't stop the plough to kill a mouse. Do not hinder important business for the discussion of a trifle.

C. H. Spurgeon

He has made everything appropriate in its time. He has also put eternity in their hearts, but man cannot discover the work God has done from beginning to end.

Ecclesiastes 3:11 Holman CSB

Today's Prayer

Dear Lord, You have given us a wonderful gift: time here on earth. Let us use it wisely—for the glory of Your kingdom and the betterment of Your world—today and every day. Amen

The World . . . and You

Don't copy the behavior and customs of this world,
but let God transform you into a new person
by changing the way you think.

Romans 12:2 NLT

We live in the world, but we must not worship it. Our duty is to place God first and everything else second. But because we are fallible beings with imperfect faith, placing God in His rightful place is often difficult. In fact, at every turn, or so it seems, we are tempted to do otherwise.

The 21st-century world is a noisy, distracting place filled with countless opportunities to stray from God's will. The world seems to cry out to you and your family, "Worship me with your time, your money, your energy, and your thoughts!" But God commands otherwise: He instructs you to worship Him and to love your neighbors; everything else must be secondary.

The world's treasures are difficult to find and difficult to keep; God's treasures are ever-present and everlasting. Which treasures, then, will you claim as your own?

The only ultimate disaster that can befall us, I have come to realize, is to feel ourselves to be home on earth.

Max Lucado

Because the world is deceptive, it is dangerous. The world can even deceive God's own people and lead them into trouble.

Warren Wiersbe

A fish would never be happy living on land, because it was made for water. An eagle could never feel satisfied if it wasn't allowed to fly. You will never feel completely satisfied on earth, because you were made for more.

Rick Warren

Better a little with the fear of the Lord than great treasure with turmoil.

Proverbs 15:16 Holman CSB

Today's Prayer

Dear Lord, I am an imperfect human being living in an imperfect world. Direct my path far from the temptations and distractions of this world, and let me follow in the footsteps of Your Son today and forever. Amen

Thanking God for His Blessings

Thanks be to God for His indescribable gift.

2 Corinthians 9:15 Holman CSB

If you and your spouse sat down and began counting your blessings, how long would it take? A very, very long time! Your blessings include life, freedom, family, friends, talents, and possessions, for starters. But, your greatest blessing—a gift that is yours for the asking—is God's gift of salvation through Christ Jesus.

Today, give thanks for your blessings by accepting them fully (with open arms) and by sharing them generously (with a thankful heart).

Billy Graham had this advice: "Think of the blessings we so easily take for granted: Life itself; preservation from danger; every bit of health we enjoy; every hour of liberty; the ability to see, to hear, to speak, to think, and to imagine all this comes from the hand of God." And that's sound advice for Christians—like you—who have been blessed beyond measure.

The words "thank" and "think" come from the same root word. If we would think more, we would thank more.

Warren Wiersbe

Why wait until the fourth Thursday in November? Why wait until the morning of December twenty-fifth? Thanksgiving to God should be an everyday affair. The time to be thankful is now!

Jim Gallery

The heathen misrepresent God by worshipping idols; we misrepresent God by our murmuring and our complaining.

C. H. Spurgeon

A virtuous woman is a crown to her husband . . . .

Proverbs 12:4 KJV

Today's Prayer

Heavenly Father, Your gifts are greater than we can imagine. Let us live each day with thanksgiving in our hearts and praise on our lips. Thank You for the gift of Your Son and for the promise of eternal life. Today and every day, let us share the joyous news of Jesus Christ, and let our lives be testimonies to His love and His grace. Amen

The Shepherd's Gift

My cup runs over. Surely goodness and mercy
shall follow me all the days of my life;
and I will dwell in the house of the Lord forever.
Psalm 23:5-6 NKJV

When we entrust our hearts and our days to the One who created us, we experience abundance through the grace and sacrifice of His Son. But, when we turn our thoughts and direct our energies away from God's commandments, we inevitably forfeit the spiritual abundance that might otherwise be ours.

Do you and your wife sincerely seek the riches that our Savior offers to those who give themselves to Him? Then follow Him completely and obey Him without reservation. When you do, you will receive the love and the abundance that He has promised. Seek first the salvation that is available through a personal relationship with Jesus Christ, and then claim the joy, the peace, and the spiritual abundance that the Shepherd offers His sheep.

People, places, and things were never meant to give us life. God alone is the author of a fulfilling life.

Gary Smalley & John Trent

Instead of living a black-and-white existence, we'll be released into a Technicolor world of vibrancy and emotion when we more accurately reflect His nature to the world around us.

Bill Hybels

And God is able to make every grace overflow to you, so that in every way, always having everything you need, you may excel in every good work.

2 Corinthians 9:8 Holman CSB

Today's Prayer

Dear Lord, as my wife and I travel through this life together, we will travel with You. Whatever this day may bring, we will thank You for the opportunity to live abundantly. We will lean upon You, Father—and trust You—this day and forever. Amen

Unbending Truth

*So put away all falsehood and "tell your neighbor the truth"
because we belong to each other.*

Ephesians 4:25 NLT

Oswald Chambers advised, "Never support an experience which does not have God as its source, and faith in God as its result." These words serve as a powerful reminder that as Christian men, we are called to walk with God and to obey His commandments. But, we live in a world that presents us with countless temptations to wander far from God's path. These temptations have the potential to destroy us, in part, because they cause us to be dishonest with ourselves and with others.

Dishonesty is a habit. Once we start bending the truth, we're likely to keep bending it. A far better strategy, of course, is to acquire the habit of being completely forthright with God, with other people, and with ourselves.

Honesty is also a habit, a habit that pays powerful dividends for those who place character above convenience. So, the next time you're tempted to bend the truth—or to break it—ask yourself this simple question:

"What does God want to do?" Then listen carefully to your conscience. When you do, your actions will be honorable, and your character will take care of itself.

A person's character is determined by his motives, and motive is always a matter of the heart.

John Eldredge

Character is formed by doing the thing we are supposed to do, when it should be done, whether we feel like doing it or not.

Father Flanagan

A solid trust is based on a consistent character.

John Maxwell

A good name is to be chosen rather than great riches, loving favor rather than silver and gold.

Proverbs 22:1 NKJV

Today's Prayer

Heavenly Father, my wife deserves a husband who is a man of integrity. Help me see the truth, help me speak the truth, and help me live the truth—today and every day of my life. Amen

A Fresh Opportunity

If anyone belongs to Christ, there is a new creation. The old things have gone; everything is made new!

2 Corinthians 5:17 NCV

Each morning offers a fresh opportunity to invite Christ, yet once again, to rule over our hearts and our days. Each morning presents yet another opportunity to take up His cross and follow in His footsteps.

God's Word is clear: When we genuinely invite Him to reign over our hearts, and when we accept His transforming love, we are forever changed. When we welcome Christ into our hearts, an old life ends and a new way of living—along with a completely new way of viewing the world—begins.

Today, let us rejoice in the new life that is ours through Christ, and let us follow Him, step by step, on the path that He first walked.

When I met Christ, I felt that I had swallowed sunshine.

E. Stanley Jones

No man is ever the same after God has laid His hand upon him.

A. W. Tozer

The transforming love of God has repositioned me for eternity. I am now a new man, forgiven, basking in the warm love of our living God, trusting His promises and provision, and enjoying life to the fullest.

Bill Bright

Turn your life over to Christ today, and your life will never be the same.

Billy Graham

Whoever believes that Jesus is the Christ is born of God, and whoever loves the Father loves the child born of Him.

1 John 5:1 NASB

Today's Prayer

Heavenly Father, renew in me the passion to share the Good News of Jesus Christ. Make the experience of my conversion real and fresh so that I might be an effective witness to my wife, to my family, and to the world. Amen

Day 99

Eternal Love, Eternal Life

Because I live, you will live also.
John 14:19 NASB

Ours is not a distant God. Ours is a God who understands—far better than we ever could—the essence of what it means to be human. How marvelous it is that God became a man and walked among us. Had He not chosen to do so, we might feel removed from a distant Creator.

God understands our hopes, our fears, and our temptations. He understands what it means to be angry and what it costs to forgive. He knows the heart, the conscience, and the soul of every person who has ever lived, including you. And God has a plan of salvation that is intended for you.

The Bible makes it clear that God's love for you and your wife is deeper and more profound than either of you can imagine. When you and your bride embrace God together, both of you are forever changed. When you embrace God's love, you feel differently about yourself, your marriage, your family, and your world. When you join together and accept God's love, the two of you will be transformed.

So, if you and your wife genuinely want to build a love that endures, make God the focus of your marriage. When you do, your marriage will last forever—and so will your love.

Those of us who know the wonderful grace of redemption look forward to an eternity with God, when all things will be made new, when all our longings will at last find ultimate and final satisfaction.

Joseph Stowell

God loves you and wants you to experience peace and life—abundant and eternal.

Billy Graham

Love never ends.

1 Corinthians 13:8 Holman CSB

Today's Prayer

We know, Lord, that this world is not our home; we are only here for a brief while. And, You have given us the priceless gift of eternal life through Your Son Jesus. Keep the hope of heaven fresh in our hearts, and, while we are in this world, help us to pass through it with faith in our hearts and praise on our lips. Amen

Commissioned to Witness

Therefore go and make disciples of all nations,
baptizing them in the name of the Father and of the Son
and of the Holy Spirit, and teaching them to obey
everything I have commanded you.
And surely I am with you always,
to the very end of the age.

Matthew 28:19-20 NIV

After His resurrection, Jesus addressed His disciples. As recorded in the 28th chapter of Matthew, Christ instructed His followers to share His message with the world. This "Great Commission" applies to Christians of every generation, including our own.

As believers, we are called to share the Good News of Jesus with our families, with our neighbors, and with the world. Christ commanded His disciples to become fishers of men. We must do likewise, and we must do so today. Tomorrow may indeed be too late.

Witnessing is not something that we do for the Lord; it is something that He does through us if we are filled with the Holy Spirit.

Warren Wiersbe

In their heart of hearts, I think all true followers of Christ long to become contagious Christians. Though unsure about how to do so or the risks involved, deep down they sense that there isn't anything as rewarding as opening a person up to God's love and truth.

Bill Hybels

You are the light of the world. A city that is set on a hill cannot be hidden. Nor do they light a lamp and put it under a basket, but on a lampstand, and it gives light to all who are in the house. Let your light so shine before men, that they may see your good works and glorify your Father in heaven.

Matthew 5:14–16 NKJV

Today's Prayer

Heavenly Father, every man and woman, every boy and girl is Your child. You desire that all Your children know Jesus as their Lord and Savior. Father, let my wife and I be part of Your Great Commission. Let us give, let us pray, and let us go out into this world so that we might be fishers of men . . . for You. Amen

If I speak the languages of men and of angels, but do not have love, I am a sounding gong or a clanging cymbal.
If I have the gift of prophecy, and understand all mysteries and all knowledge, and if I have all faith, so that I can move mountains, but do not have love, I am nothing.
And if I donate all my goods to feed the poor, and if I give my body to be burned, but do not have love, I gain nothing.
Love is patient; love is kind. Love does not envy; is not boastful; is not conceited; does not act improperly; is not selfish; is not provoked; does not keep a record of wrongs; finds no joy in unrighteousness, but rejoices in the truth; bears all things, believes all things, hopes all things, endures all things. Love never ends. But as for prophecies, they will come to an end; as for languages, they will cease; as for knowledge, it will come to an end. For we know in part, and we prophesy in part. But when the perfect comes, the partial will come to an end. When I was a child, I spoke like a child, I thought like a child, I reasoned like a child. When I became a man, I put aside childish things. For now we see indistinctly, as in a mirror, but then face to face. Now I know in part, but then I will know fully, as I am fully known.
Now these three remain: faith, hope, and love.
But the greatest of these is love.

—

1 Corinthians 13:1-13 Holman CSB